The Critical Thinking Tool Kit

The Critical Thinking Tool Kit

Spark Your Team's Creativity with 35 Problem Solving Activities

Marlene Caroselli

AMACOM

New York • Atlanta • Brussels • Chicago • Mexico City • San Francisco
Shanghai • Tokyo • Toronto • Washington, D.C.

Bulk discounts available. For details visit:
www.amacombooks.org/go/specialsales
Or contact special sales:
Phone: 800-250-5308
Email: specialsls@amanet.org
View all the AMACOM titles at: www.amacombooks.org

This publication is designed to provide accurate and authoritative information in regard to the subject matter covered. It is sold with the understanding that the publisher is not engaged in rendering legal, accounting, or other professional service. If legal advice or other expert assistance is required, the services of a competent professional person should be sought.

This is a modified version of a text previously published by HRD Press as *50 Activities for Developing Critical Thinking Skills.*

Library of Congress Cataloging-in-Publication Data

Caroselli, Marlene.
    The critical thinking tool kit : spark your team's creativity with 35
problem solving activities / Marlene Caroselli.
        p. cm.
    Includes bibliographical references and index.
    ISBN 978-0-8144-1740-9
    1. Creative ability in business.   2. Critical thinking.   3. Teams in
the workplace.   I. Title.
HD53.C376 2011
658.4′036—dc22

                                                    2011000972

About AMA
American Management Association (www.amanet.org) is a world leader in talent development, advancing the skills of individuals to drive business success. Our mission is to support the goals of individuals and organizations through a complete range of products and services, including classroom and virtual seminars, webcasts, webinars, podcasts, conferences, corporate and government solutions, business books, and research. AMA's approach to improving performance combines experiential learning—learning through doing—with opportunities for ongoing professional growth at every step of one's career journey.

Printing number
10 9 8 7 6 5 4 3 2 1

Contents

Electronic files for the Handouts, Transparencies, and Worksheets, as well as the Table of Contents and the Matrix of Exercises, are to be found at
www.amacombooks.org/go/CriticalThinking

As the economy dramatically shifts and settles, fundamental questions are being raised about the readiness of the workers to handle the jobs of the future. Is your company ready to handle international competition? Is it agile enough to deal with rapid change? What skills will the new economy require?

Traditional education with a focus on a proficiency in reading, writing, and arithmetic has worked in the past, but the new workplace requires more from its employees. Employees need to think critically, solve problems, innovate, collaborate, and communicate more effectively—and at every level within the organization. According to the *AMA 2010 Critical Skills Survey,* many executives admit there is room for improvement among their employees in these skills and competencies.

In an effort to assess how "top of mind" these skills and competencies are, the American Management Association (AMA)—in conjunction with P21, a national organization that advocates for 21st-century readiness for every student—surveyed 2,115 managers and other executives in AMA member and customer companies about the importance of the four Cs to their organization today and in the future.

The American Management Association 2010 Critical Skills Survey defined the skills as follows:

- **Critical thinking and problem solving**—the ability to make decisions, solve problems, and take action as appropriate
- **Effective communication**—the ability to synthesize and transmit your ideas both in written and oral formats
- **Collaboration and team building**—the ability to work effectively with others, including those from diverse groups and with opposing points of view
- **Creativity and innovation**—the ability to see what's NOT there and make something happen

For more information on the findings and a copy of the survey, visit http://www.amanet.org/training/articles/3727.aspx.

The Critical Thinking Tool Kit

This book is designed to help you improve the critical thinking and problem-solving abilities of your team. Complete with 35 activities and assessments to determine an employee's progress, this tool kit makes it easy for managers to quickly and effectively teach their teams how to think quickly, creatively, and analytically.

The Critical Thinking Tool Kit

Critical Thinking: "What" and "Why"

The Analysis Factor

Today's employee is bombarded with organizational oxymorons. In this age of paradox, we are expected to keep our heads above water shored by contradiction. Learning is a life long process, yet we are forced to absorb it in machine-gun bursts. Advice broken down into sound bites is offered to us constantly, yet we are asked instead to draw big pictures, envision far-off, uncertain futures, and operate from strategic, well-planned positions. We absorb facts coming at us faster than the speed of light, yet we struggle for the clarity and creativity critical if we are to make wise use of this new knowledge. And we know one thing with certainty: We have to do more with less, and we must do it in far less time.

Continuous learning and the imaginative application of it are needed if the organization itself is to continue. Imaginative thought, described by management guru Tom Peters as the "only source of real value in the new economy," originates with well-informed employees who employ critical thinking to translate knowledge into competitive advantage. By critical thinking, we refer to thought processes that are quick, accurate, and assumption-free. (They are often creative as well.) Such processes help us view, with a critical eye, the problems, decisions, and situations that require appropriate reaction and action.

"Critical," after all, is derived from the Greek word *krisis,* which means "to separate." When life presents us with turning points, when we are faced with situations that require decisive action, when we need plans that will yield positive consequences, then we also need critical thinking. Such thinking allows us to separate ourselves from the crisis that can suck us into disaster and permits us, instead, to forge new pathways to success.

Non-traditional thinking, grounded in traditional, logical thought, enables us to determine exactly what the crisis is and how to move beyond it. Let us use this true story involving a medical crisis as an example.

A middle-aged man called his doctor in the middle of the night. He described the pains his wife was having, diagnosed them as appendicitis (which he himself had experienced), and told the doctor he was bringing the woman into emergency.

The doctor, however, was much less concerned. He diagnosed the problem as stomach cramps, advised the man to give her ginger ale, and suggested that an appointment be made in the morning for an office visit. The man, fortunately, persisted.

Not used to having his medical judgment questioned, the doctor spoke authoritatively: "It *cannot* be her appendix," he declared. "I distinctly remember removing your wife's appendix eight years ago. And I have never heard of a woman having a second appendix!"

Before hanging up and driving his wife to the hospital, the man shot back, "Did you ever hear of a man having a second wife?"

Had the doctor thought more critically, he would have realized the flaws in his logic. He would have used the basic precept on which rational thought is based: The Principle of Identity.

This principle would have led him to accept the logic of the statement that no woman can have two appendixes, and then to question the identity of the woman. Had he done so, he would have not only accepted his own statement as true, but would have realized that a second woman could have that second appendix.

Another principle, The Principle of Excluded Middles, asserts that a statement is either true or false—it cannot be both. Thinking about "excluded middles" will help us examine the statements we make and the attitudes we possess, the very fixedness of which can prevent us from solving problems and actually create new ones. A statement like "Leaders such as Adolf Hitler effect positive change" cannot be simultaneously both true and false. This statement is actually predicated on two separate premises, the second of which is questionable:

1. Leaders effect positive change.
2. Adolf Hitler was a leader.

Critical thinking about these two statements requires us to define what is meant by the word "leader" and then to determine if the example of Hitler falls within the established criteria. Critical thinking also requires us to clarify terms that not only confuse but that may create expensive misunderstandings. This sentence, for example, has two possible meanings:

"Your consultant may not charge a fee for his or her location services."

The phrase "may not" could mean "is not permitted to." It could also mean, however, "may not opt to charge a fee, although he or she *could* charge one if he or she wished to."

The Creativity Factor

More than logical, linear thought is required when change slams us into the wall labeled "no established precedent." Non-traditional thinking is required to create the non-traditional systems needed for the non-typical situations that present themselves with ever-increasing rapidity. There are times when breakthrough thinking is the only force that can move us beyond the mundane and into the rarefied stratum of true innovation. With logical thought, we analyze what is there. With creative thought, we contemplate what *isn't* there. "Vision" was defined by Jonathan Swift as "the art of seeing the invisible."

Imagination is what takes vision out of its tunnel. And once freed from a confining place, vision can become an innovation-driven reality. Creative thought is not the private domain of the rare few who are able to see something new when others look at something old. Rather, each of us has an unlimited reservoir of creative potential. Unfortunately, as we mature, we manage to surrender our remarkable ability to envision, an ability Einstein himself regarded as more important than knowledge.

To illustrate, a famous longitudinal study of creative potential followed a group of students over a 17-year period. The *same test* was administered each time to these students. When the students were five years old, 92% of them were found to be "very creative." By age ten, that figure had dropped to 37%. When the children were fifteen, they were tested again. At this age, the number of children deemed "very creative" had dropped to 12%. Finally, the same students were tested in college. How many were found to be "very creative" at this age? Only 2%!

Critical thinkers use both types of thinking, depending on the demands of the situation. The ideal is to be "lateralized" in your thought processes, meaning that you can employ either type of cognition equally well.

Creative thinkers are able to leave behind perfectly logical answers that, unfortunately, are not solving the problems. Instead of persevering, trying to force-fit a round solution into a square problem, such thinkers are willing to explore a different approach. Creative thinkers are risk-takers.

A simple exercise will illustrate what we mean. The following combination of letters represents a sentence from which one particular vowel has been removed. If you can figure out what that vowel is and re-insert it eleven times, in eleven different places, you will be able to determine what the sentence is saying.

VRYFINXMP
LARXCDSW
HATWXPCT

Most problem-solvers soon realize the missing letter is "e," probably because the word "very" seems to jump out at them. They work very hard to construct the sentence with "very" as its first word. "Very" is *not* the first word, however; "every" is. When conviction and determination prevent us from exploring alternative options, we limit our potential for thinking critically. (The whole sentence reads, "Every fine exemplar exceeds what we expect.")

The Speed Factor

Caught in the middle of a veritable knowledge explosion, we find, more than ever before, that (s)he who hesitates may indeed be lost. With amazing frequency, individuals are showing a reluctance, for example, to use so-called snail-mail to transmit their thoughts when electronic mail can connect us with people halfway around the world in mere seconds. This reluctance has its parallel in organizations wary of employing those whose thinking processes move at a snail's pace.

Tom Peters likes to point out that in 1985, a typical memory chip held a million bits of information. In less than a decade, the number had increased to sixteen million. Projections for the year 2030 include 16 terabits or 16 *trillion* bits of information. As he in his inimitably down-to-earth vernacular expresses it, "We ain't seen nothin' yet."

Speed in and of itself is a necessary, but not sufficient, condition for critical thought. It must be supplemented with either creative or analytical thought—and sometimes with both. Hasty reactions unaccompanied by deliberate thought can have disastrous results at both personal and corporate levels.

The Benefits of Critical Thinking

When crises arise in our personal or professional lives, we are often required to respond quickly. The quick response, however, is always predicated on accurately identifying the problem. Such attention to the input enhances the likelihood that outputs will be positive. This focus on improved outcomes that are faster, better, cheaper, and of higher quality is what continuous improvement is all about.

Management studies underscore the need to develop our collective smarts. Consider the following:

> *A recent report by Kepner-Tregoe, Inc., found that two-thirds of managers and hourly workers estimated that less than 50% of their collective brainpower was being used by the organizations for which they worked.*

In the Kepner-Tregoe study cited above, only 8% of managers and 7% of hourly workers would compare their organizational thinking to a Ferrari, in terms of quality and speed. However, there is a renewed interest in the subject of learning today. Individuals, teams, and whole institutions are devoting themselves to sharpening cerebral skills. The need to think critically is truly a valuable commodity. In some respects, it is a necessity.

This book is designed for decision-makers and problem-solvers who don't always have the luxury of advance preparation.

Given sufficient lead time, most of us could prepare responses or presentations reflective of our abilities, and come up with replies and responses worthy of our backgrounds and training. But what happens when we are called upon to make a statement "on the spot," to make a decision without having all the facts, to solve a problem that will only be exacerbated by delay? Often, we become paralyzed by the urgency of the moment. Our thought processes stop. Our organizational abilities abandon us. But the ability to think quickly and speak quickly formulated thoughts is not an innate ability. *It can be developed.* The exercises in this book parallel Lee Iacocca's advice to would-be executives: "The best thing you can do for your career is learn to think on your feet."

The collection included in this book also emphasizes creative thinking, and stresses communication skills in keeping with recent research findings. Consultant Andrew Sherwood considers communication and financial knowledge the most valuable of all workplace skills.

Running through the fabric of all these activities, though, are problem-solving threads. Dr. Roger Flax surveyed 1,000 executives and found that the skills most needed among employees were problem-solving, writing, and time management, in that order. It's been said that at the most basic level, everything comes together; it is all intellectually integrated, if we regard life as a series of problems to be solved. Quick thinking, creative thinking, and problem-solving skills *all* help us to think critically.

Format of the Book

The three most important aspects of critical thinking—quick thinking, creative thinking, and analytical thinking—are covered by a series of skill-building exercises.

Quick Thinking. What enables one person to respond to an unexpected prompt fluidly and flawlessly, while another person stumbles and mumbles and fumbles for words? Often the distinguishing factor is that one person does not practice thinking on one's feet, while another person does. The practice exercises in this section are useful, but they are also entertaining. They will develop critical thinking skills—especially important in those situations that force us to keep our wits about us.

Creative Thinking. Unfortunately, many perfectly able problem-solvers damn themselves by declaring that they are not creative and should not be expected to come up with creative solutions. The truth is that we all have creative potential. We may have allowed the potential to be submerged, but it lies within us, nonetheless. The exercises in this section show participants how to strip away layers of self-doubt, self-criticism, and self-cynicism in order to rediscover their creative cores.

Analytical Thinking. Despite the plethora of problems confronting us on a daily basis, few of us have had formal training in problem-solving. The exercises in this section employ tools for solving problems logically (based on the scientific approach of defining the problem, generating a list of possible solutions, selecting a solution, and then implementing, evaluating, and making adjustments as needed). The Five-Why tool will force us as problem-solvers to uncover the root cause of the problem, which will lead to a solution that permits expedient and results-oriented action.

For Quick Reference

This matrix sequences the activities as you will encounter them in each of the three sections, specifies the amount of time required for each of the three sections, and specifies the amount of time required for each activity, in terms of minutes. The basic construct of the activities is depicted as well: Individual assignments call for reflection and self-assessments; Tasks for Pairs require participants to work as partners. There are also Small Group exercises, in which three or four participants tackle a problem or challenge together. Finally, there are Large Group activities, asking six or more participants to collaborate.

The Letter "P" designates the need for advance preparation, which is minimal in all cases. The typical advance preparation involves the duplication of materials and the arrangement of seats in ways that are most conducive to participant involvement.

Quick Thinking

Time (min.)	Exercise	Individual	Pair	Small Group	Large Group
15	Attending to Attention			P	
25	Rhymed Reductions				P
15	The Endless Question		P		
20	The Questionable Question				
15	The K-W-I-C Technique	P			
15	Juxtaposed Pairs			P	
25	Presidential Pairs				P
20	The Umbrage Not Taken		P		
20	Brainteasing/Brainsqueezing	P			
10	Perceptual Shifts	P			
25	Organizational Oxymorons			P	
25	Stratification			P	

Creative Thinking

Time (min.)	Exercise	Individual	Pair	Small Group	Large Group
15	Particular Virtues				P
15	Perspicacious Perspectives				
15	Turnarounds			P	
25	Left Is Right. So Is Right.		P		
25	Ms. Matches and Mr. Matches	P			
20	Cre8—GetN2It			P	
15	Think Outside the Locks				P
15	Thinking Is an Art	P			
15	A Kin to Kinesthesia			P	
10	Low and High Logos			P	
15	Blues on Parade		P		
20	Scrambled Pegs		P		

Analytical Thinking

Time (min.)	Exercise	Individual	Pair	Small Group	Large Group
35	Crisis Critiques			P	
25	Trend-Spotters			P	
30	The Triple-A Approach				P
20	A Foolery of Fun		P		
20	Patterned Organization		P		
15	Pro Con'd				P
25	Direct Responses				P
20	In Your Sights				
20	Giving Problems a Why'd Berth				P
25	Resource-Full			P	
15	Living Problems, Lively Solutions				

Format of the Exercises

Each activity begins with an *Overview* or brief explanation of what the activity entails and its significance for critical thinkers.

This is followed by the *Objective,* which is written as an answer to the question, "What does this activity do?" Objectives are typically written from the facilitator's or the participant's perspective, but we have chosen to write these as clear statements of purpose.

The *Supplies* listed in the third entry are standard supplies for adult learning situations, inexpensive and readily available in most training rooms.

The *Time* listed is an approximation; it may vary according to the number of participants and their levels of expertise. Allow additional time for optional extended activities (designed to reinforce key points), or when using the debriefing questions that appear at the end of each activity. The activities can be expanded to considerably longer periods when these two optional elements are built in.

Complicated or excessive *Advance Preparations* sometimes discourage a facilitator from using specific activities. For this reason, activities have deliberately been kept simple and user-friendly.

The *Participants/Applications* section provides information on the ideal number of participants and the most appropriate times and places for the activity within the instructional sequence.

The actual lessons begin with an *Introduction to Concept.* These mini-lectures contain background information that permits easy transitions to the concepts being presented. They contain the text the facilitator can use or paraphrase to introduce the lesson. Examples are provided throughout the Introductions when illustrations are required.

The *Procedure* is a sequential listing of the steps to be followed as the activity is conducted. As simply as possible, the facilitator is given information essential to each exercise in order to maximize the effectiveness of the instructions.

Included in the *Procedure* are suggestions for *Extending the Activity.* These will help reinforce the concept being presented or the skill being reinforced, and can be used immediately following the activity or at a later time as a review or refresher exercise.

Workplace Connections are suggestions for extending the learning beyond the classroom. They encourage the facilitator and the participant to apply the lessons learned to other situations and expand upon the basic concepts presented.

Questions for Further Consideration have been included at the end of each activity in order to strengthen the application between training and the actual work that attendees do when they return to their offices or workplaces. The questions can be asked by the facilitator before the session begins (the list could be sent to attendees several days prior to the start of the course), during the session, or at the end of the session as a means of debriefing and achieving closure. Ideally attendees will continue to ask and answer these questions long after the training program itself has concluded. Three distinct groups of people within any organization will benefit from this book:

1. Trainers will enrich their presentations by including fast-paced, interactive exercises that stimulate both thought and group cohesiveness, regardless of the topic of the meeting or lecture.

2. Learners will benefit from exposure to a wide array of strategies for framing problems and formulating solutions.

3. Organizations will profit because improved thinking on the part of employees always leads to improved contributions. Intellectual capital that is not capitalized on represents the losses to which Dr. W. Edwards Deming refers: "The greatest losses are unknown and unknowable."

Adaptability of This Book

Although this book was designed with the manager or corporate trainer/facilitator in mind, the activities lend themselves to other settings (from academic settings to the adult training programs offered by public and private businesses). We encourage you to share them with others, whether they sit before you as learners or beside you as co-workers.

To paraphrase Thomas Mann: "The activity, even the most challenging activity, brings us together. It is silence that isolates." I first alluded to the need for verbal connectedness nearly twenty years ago, when I left education for a new life and a new career on the West Coast. I wrote then in *The New York State English Record,* "Those of us who are leaving education, temporarily or permanently, may feel a need to break the 'chain reaction' of which Neruda speaks in *Goodbyes:*

> *I spread myself, no question;*
> *I turned over whole lives,*
> *changed skin, lamps, and hates,*
> *it was something I had to do,*
> *not by law or whim,*
> *more of a chain reaction..."*

This collection was also something I *had to do.* It permits me to say "Hello" again.

Overview:	This activity provides participants with a means of efficiently encoding information by using a framework with which to organize important information in a meaningful way.
Objective:	To provide an opportunity for participants to process information more efficiently.
Supplies:	Copies of Handout #1-1
Time:	15–20 minutes
Advance Preparation:	Make enough copies of Handout #1-1 for the entire group. Arrange the seating so it is easy for groups of three or four to share their responses.
Participants/ Application:	This activity works with any number of participants and is especially useful when one must take notes on significant material presented by a facilitator in a lecture format. It can be used each time a lecture (or mini-lecture) is presented.

Introduction to Concept:

"Tomorrow's illiterate," Herbert Gerjuoy asserts, "will not be the man who cannot read; he will be the man who has not learned how to learn." An important part of the learning process is paying attention to material we are putting into our storage banks. If we are not concentrating, if we are bored, or if we are anxious or distracted, tired or ill, depressed or excited, we may not be giving the knowledge the attention it deserves. Later, when we go to retrieve it, we will probably have difficulty finding it. When there are gaps in our knowledge, there will be corresponding gaps in our ability to critically assess situations.

When we are missing information we need, we tend to blame a "poor memory." The real culprit is an inefficient coding system. Inefficiency in this system obviates efficiency in critical thinking, for we cannot give issues a 360-degree scrutiny if we only have a 180-degree perspective.

One of the best examples of an efficient coding system is found in what is called the "skeleton image."

Procedure:

1. Introduce the Knowledge Skeleton via this presentation:

   As you prepare to listen to a lecture on "empowerment," imagine that the head and each of the limbs of a skeleton represent five large areas within this broad topic. While you listen to my lecture, make notes in one of these five areas and do not—I repeat—do not try to copy every word I say. Instead, record main points as concisely as you can.

   Look at these knowledge skeletons now. [Distribute copies of Handout #1-1, one per participant.] *Note that the areas for this topic are Business Practices, Definition of empowerment, Structures, Ideas, and Partnerships. With other topics, other areas would be significant. The next time you are in a class, ask your instructor for such an overview so you can easily add "flesh" (your notes, your thoughts) to the bare-bones outline you have been presented with.*

2. Distribute Handout #1-1 showing the knowledge skeleton and ask participants to add "flesh" to the bones by writing down important points from the lecture.

3. Read the following aloud:

   The Quality movement has forced organizations to examine current business practices, to make changes in work processes, and to create new alliances with customers, employees, and other organizations. This movement has made leadership a practice in which anyone, at any level of the organization, can engage. In the words of author Masaaki Imai of Toyota, the new leadership is based on personal experience and conviction and "not necessarily on authority, rank, or age."

   As we think about the definition of empowerment, we cannot ignore the experience and commitment of employees. When the organization acknowledges these traits and when the organization willingly uses the talents employees are eager to share, then we have a culture of empowerment.

   *Structures (formal and informal) must be in place, however, so employees' voices can be heard. In smaller companies, the top executives invite groups of employees to have lunch with them each week so they can get closer to workers and their concerns. Senior managers in empowered organizations **earnestly** seek information about problems employees may be experiencing and ideas they may have for improvement.*

   Other companies seek to "hear" employee voices by using suggestion systems. Organizations that have established formal Quality Councils already have in place the structures necessary for translating a team's well-researched proposal into feasible plans. To be sure, there will be barriers standing in the way of moving ideas from teams to managers to reality. But once these barriers have been identified, team members can work to remove them.

   It is imperative that managers actively solicit ideas from subordinates through formal suggestion processes or in less formal ways. Management cannot ignore the potential wealth of ideas waiting to be shared at every level of the organization. As Imai notes in his book Kaizen, *in one year alone, 1.5 million suggestions were offered, 95% of which were implemented fully or in part by Toyota management.*

When employees feel empowered, they get excited about the possibility of forming new partnerships. These alliances may be made with other organizations through benchmarking. They can also be made with other employees through process improvement teams, with customers through focus groups, with the community at large through new outreach programs. The form of the partnership follows the function of continuous improvement, no matter the forum.

4. Have participants compare the notes they made and discuss the content of the lecture.

5. After five minutes, ask them to put their notes away as you give a quiz:

    a. What do you remember about *business practices?*
    b. What do you remember about the *definition of empowerment?*
    c. What do you remember about *structures?*
    d. What do you remember about *ideas?*
    e. What do you remember about *partnerships?*

6. Ask them to discuss the advantages of taking notes in skeletal fashion as opposed to taking no notes or taking notes in a more haphazard way. For most people, the flesh-to-bones process works quite well. Have participants evaluate it in terms of their recall.

Extending the Activity:

1. Draw the skeleton on a flip chart and label each of the limbs and the head with one of the objectives of the course. (Or use the basic knowledge categories into which you have divided the course.) At the end of the session, have participants write what they remember having learned in each of the categories listed.

2. Preview a video you intend to show in a future class and draw the skeletal divisions on a transparency. Have participants add the flesh of ideas and new knowledge after they have viewed the film.

Workplace Connections:

1. Suggest that employees use the Knowledge Skeleton in this way when they return to work: At their next (and subsequent) staff meeting, a volunteer will keep notes of the meeting's progress by correlating the skeletal frame to the agenda for the meeting. Minutes could later be distributed—not in their usual typed format, but rather with "bulleted" entries beneath each of the focal points of the meeting.

2. Encourage the use of this framework for individual reading. Before participants begin reading a book or long magazine article, they should skim the Table of Contents or major headings to get an overarching sense of the key points being made. Then, as they are reading, they can add verbal flesh to the skeletal outlines they have prepared.

3. Reinforce the concept and process of efficient encoding by asking participants to think about the one person in their work environment whom they most admire for his or her ability to absorb and retain voluminous amounts of information. Point out that they could learn quite a bit from that individual about the mechanism this person uses to remember important information. Suggest that they invite the person to have coffee or lunch one day and initiate a conversation about this post-session assignment they have been given.

Questions for Further Consideration:

1. You have spent many years acquiring and reusing information. What mechanisms have you developed to efficiently organize and retain information?

2. It is said that the amount of "information pressure" we now experience is at least 30 times as great as it was in the 1980s. What will you do to keep up?

3. In what other areas of your life have you learned to streamline information—processes, paperwork, filing, etc.?

4. Has technology helped you efficiently store and quickly retrieve information, or has it made the process even more complicated? Explain your answer.

The Knowledge Skeleton

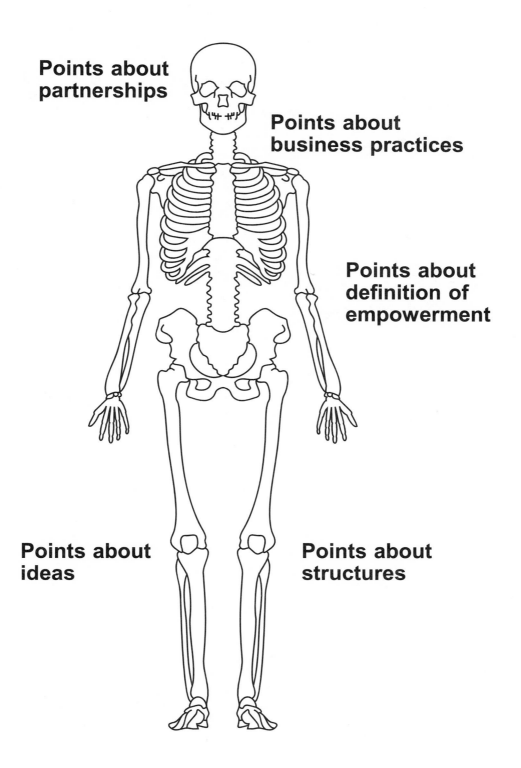

Points about partnerships

Points about business practices

Points about definition of empowerment

Points about ideas

Points about structures

Overview:
Participants will first work on a brief illustrative activity via an overhead transparency and will engage in a longer activity, in teams, to analyze a lengthy passage and reduce it to its simplest terms.

Objective:
To stimulate critical assessment and the ability to translate excessive information into valuable nuggets of knowledge.

Supplies:
- Transparency #2-1
- Overhead projector
- Copies of Handout #2-1

Time:
About 25 minutes

Advance Preparation:
Download Transparency #2-1. Also make copies of Handout #2-1 (enough for each participant) and staple the two pages together. If possible, arrange tables and chairs in groupings of five or six.

Participants/ Application:
This exercise, suitable for any number of participants, works especially well as an introduction to the course. It serves to remind attendees to take notes—not on every single word they hear, but rather on the points they have deemed, through a critical-thought process, to be most important. It can also be used as an energizer.

The exercise works well as a summarizing activity. Point out that the average person speaks about 150 words a minute. If they multiply that number by the number of minutes during which they have spoken, others have spoken, a video was presented, or material was read, thousands and thousands of words have entered their minds in a single day. Ask what they judge to be most valuable to them.

Introduction to Concept:

Students of psychology know that Zipf's Law of Least Effort promotes the condensing of knowledge: the more effort required to express a thought, the less likely that thought will be expressed. And, of course, when thoughts are not expressed—inwardly or outwardly—they cease to exist. Added to this cognitive thrust is William James's assertion that the essence of genius is "to know what to overlook."

This advice is echoed by author Mitchell Posner, who urges us to become "information ecologists"—individuals who keep their mental environment free of garbage (unreliable, irrelevant, or redundant information). Given the amount of information to which we have access on a daily basis, it becomes more and more important for us to find our way amid the overflow and the overload of data.

Examples:

1. Deliver the following instructions:

   I am going to show you on the overhead projector a paragraph that tells a story. I am going to flash it very quickly, so you will have to skip over most of the words and let only the truly important words penetrate your consciousness. You will feel uncomfortable doing this at first. But as you become used to the technique, you will grow more and more appreciative of the efficiency it produces.

   Look at this paragraph, but now select only the key words, so you can tell me what the gist of the paragraph is. [Show Transparency #2-1 now for three or four seconds.]

2. Ask the class if, after only a few seconds' exposure to the paragraph, anyone is able to distill its essence. If someone can, offer the appropriate praise and ask that person how he or she learned to read so efficiently. If no one is able to paraphrase the key point, show the transparency again and underline these key words or phrases:

   "Manhattan," "deceptively simple home," "deceptively simple man,"
   "Mr. Cowles," and **"evil."**

3. Continue with this mini-lecture:

   In the example, we reduced the verbiage to a few essential phrases. In longer passages, such as the one I am about to show you, you can still improve your comprehension, storage, and retrieval of information by reducing a dense passage to its most critical components. In the second exercise, I am going to ask you to reduce the essential points to **four** *words—and I want you to make them rhyming words!*

4. Distribute Handout #2-1. After participants have had enough time to read it, divide them into groups of five or six and allow about ten minutes for them to capture the essence of the passage in just four rhyming words.

5. Call on each group to share what has been done.

6. Summarize the lesson by pointing out that hundreds of books have been written over the years on the topic of teams and teambuilding, yet most people recall very little of what was read. Those who do are likely to use a four-word rhyming phrase coined more than thirty years ago by consultant Bruce Tuckman to describe the stages of team formation (which is basically what the handout described). The four stages are Form–Storm–Norm–Perform. Everyone remembers Mr. Tuckman's condensation. And with this four-word embryo, most people can then expound upon the nature of teams and the dynamics evinced by team members.

   [**Note:** If class members are already familiar with Bruce Tuckman's descriptors, have them select four other rhyming words that are equally effective at capturing the salient points of the passage.]

Extending the Activity:

1. Take a newspaper article and use it to engage participants in the same process. Ask them to reduce the paragraphs to a few salient points—rhyming ones at that. Several hours or several days later (depending on the length of the course), supply them with the rhyming words and ask them to recall the details of the article from which they were derived.

2. Collect other examples of how a synthesized version made the longer version much easier to remember. Encourage class members to do the same. Have a volunteer distribute examples to class members and discuss them.

3. Instead of information on team formation, select lengthy textbook passages of material relevant to the course you are facilitating, and ask participants to reduce the information to the most essential knowledge.

Workplace Connections:

1. Before the training session has ended, ask for a group of volunteers to review at least one instructional or user's manual to see if important steps can be reduced to an easy-to-remember memory trigger.

2. Advise participants to work collaboratively when they return to work in order to help one another become more skilled at using rhyme or other mnemonic devices as prompts to recall large chunks of information they are expected to have at their fingertips.

3. Ad writers are especially adept at conveying the most meaning in the fewest possible words. Ask participants to rewrite their organization's mission statement (which few people, typically, can recall) into an easy-to-remember phrase (or advertisement) that captures the essential thrust of the statement.

Questions for Further Consideration:

1. What slogans or advertisements come quickly to mind? Why?

2. Speed readers know that 90% of the time, the main idea of a paragraph is contained in the first line of the paragraph. Thus, they are able to skim newspaper or magazine articles and understand the gist of the message without spending undue amounts of time absorbing the facts. What other techniques do speed-readers and speed-comprehenders employ?

3. Management guru Peter Drucker coined the phrase "knowledge workers" to describe the American workforce as it evolved from an industrial economy to a service economy. What evidence do you have that we are dependent upon the sharing of knowledge, organization-ally, nationally, and globally, more than ever before?

4. Do you ever feel you are drowning in a sea of information? What can you do to overcome this feeling?

5. What can organizations do to help employees cope with information overload?

In the middle of a long, tree-lined street in a quiet residential neighborhood in that oft-praised metropolis known world 'round as Manhattan stood a deceptively simple home. Its simplicity was belied by the exquisite detail that had been devoted to its gardens, reminiscent of English labyrinth walkways. Inside the home lived a deceptively simple man known to his neighbors as Mr. Cowles—known to his victims as "Evil."

The Natural Evolution of Teams

When team members first convene as a group, they come to the meeting with considerable trepidation. They are really not certain what they can expect. They turn to the leader for information, for guidelines, for introductions, and so on. At this stage, team members are guarded, uncertain, not willing to reveal much about themselves. They are filled with questions but probably not willing to ask them. Their behavior is polite, but not really congenial. They are probably experiencing some nervous tension. The leader must work hard at the beginning to thaw the cold exteriors that strangers typically show one another.

As the meeting progresses (or perhaps by the second meeting), members begin to open up. Along with this openness, however, comes a willingness to disagree. As time goes on, members seem more willing to rebel against decisions that go against their individual grain. In this second stage, there will frequently be confrontations, which are to be expected if the team is to learn about its composite membership and grow as a unit. The team leader lets eruptions occur in this stage, but does not let them get out of control. He or she allows others to take leadership positions as the occasion warrants. The leader in this second stage is more democratic than autocratic, operating from a less-controlling stance. He or she, however, does not completely relinquish authority. The leader works hard to achieve group harmony.

The third stage in the evolution of teams is marked by the beginning of commitment. Team members start to offer their talents; they recognize the importance of the task before them. The leader consults with members and willingly shares the leadership role. The importance of the task starts to override the importance of individual needs as members become more committed. Team members now begin to find ways to accomplish their shared task more efficiently. They agree to abide by common ground rules. They exhibit a desire to share, to experiment. The pride they are beginning to feel in their accomplishment is matched by the enthusiasm they feel for the mission and for the opportunity to work together.

The final stage of teambuilding represents the idealized version of the process. The leader has virtually abdicated his or her role, now serving primarily as mentor or resource. As the team becomes more self-directed, the leader essentially works as an equal member. The team leader knows the team has become powerful as an entity and that he or she can relinquish power as a leader. Team members at this stage care about one another; they display commitment to the common goal; they cooperate. Their disagreements are caused by concern for the goal rather than concern for self-aggrandizement. At this stage, team members demonstrate that they have learned how to give and take criticism. They enjoy working with one another and can see the light of accomplishment at the end of their common tunnel. They are living proof that "united we stand; divided we fall."

Overview: Whether one is in a job interview ("womb-to-tomb" employment is no longer a realistic possibility for most of us) or is simply asked an unexpected question, quick-wittedness is a valuable skill to have. This activity, a challenging one, helps participants gain a few extra thinking moments by asking a question instead of giving an immediate answer. The question will often elicit the kind of information needed in order to respond in a cogent, albeit quick, manner. It also allows us time to gather our thoughts.

Objective: To provide participants with a tool for responding quickly and intelligently to unanticipated prompts.

Supplies:
- Copies of Handout #3-1
- Token prizes or certificates (optional)

Time: 15–20 minutes

Advance Preparation: Make copies of Handout #3-1, one per participant. If possible, arrange seating so that each participant can easily converse with a partner. Invite a member of senior management to serve as judge. You may also wish to buy token prizes or prepare certificates to award to the winning pair.

Participants/ Application: This exercise can be used as an icebreaker at the beginning of the session or as an energizer at any point during the session. It is also adaptable to a wide range of programs, such as communication, leadership, and interviewing. It can be used with any number of participants. If there is an extra person left after all the pairs have been formed, he or she can also serve as the judge.

Introduction to Concept:

The ability to think quickly, according to business leader Lee Iacocca, is the most vital element of career success. James Hayes of the American Management Association similarly asserts that "leaders who are inarticulate make us all uneasy." When we see our organizational or national leaders falter in a debate or crumble before a reporter's probing questions, we begin to lose faith in their ability to lead. Just as we expect our leaders to be able to think on their feet, so are *we* expected to exhibit verbal grace under pressure, in all sorts of personal and professional situations. (If you've ever watched the crowning of Miss America, you know how important this ability can be.)

This exercise truly requires quick-wittedness, as every remark must be interrogative.

Example:

It may sound easy to you at first, but the challenge to answer every question with another question is a formidable one, indeed. Here is an example of how it works. (Notice that none of the questions use the convenient tag line, "Isn't it?" at the end of a declarative statement. Try to avoid this easy way out, and avoid responses that do not logically flow from the preceding question.)

Person A:	"Why do you think we are doing this assignment?"
Person B:	"Have you ever heard of anything like this?"
Person A:	"Have you?"
Person B:	"Isn't this similar to 'Verbal Volley?'"
Person A:	"What's that?"
Person B:	"Haven't you ever heard of it?"
Person A:	"Didn't I just indicate that I haven't?"
Person B:	"Have I offended you somehow?"
Person A:	"Do you think I could be offended by a question?"

Procedure:

1. Have participants form pairs. (If one is left over, he or she can either work with you in this exchange of questions or serve as a roving judge to select the finalists in the competition.)

2. Allow them a few minutes practice in preparing a dialogue with as many questions as possible in it.

3. The four pairs with the greatest number of questions will come to the front of the room and, one pair at a time, will engage in another question-exchange using a prompt that the judge(s) supplies. The judge(s) may begin by asking the first team one of these questions:

   How are you feeling today?
   What's happening in your life?
   What do you think about the economy?
   What do you like best about this month?
   What advice would you give to new employees coming to work here?
   What do you like best about your job?

   The judge(s) may elect to ask a different question. The two members of the pair use the question to start the round of verbal-volleying. A volunteer should be asked to tally the number of questions each pair asks. After the first team finishes, the next begins.

4. After the winners have been determined, ask each participant to select a new partner. Then distribute Handout #3-1. Each person will ask one question from his or her partner's list. Before the partner begins to respond, he or she should ask just one question in order to gain a few moments for gathering thoughts. Once he or she receives a reply to this one question, he or she can respond to it without interrogative statements.

Extending the Activity:

1. A similar exercise can be done using other types of sentences; words related to the program being presented should appear in each sentence.

2. Make a collection of unusual questions participants have been asked in interview situations. Periodically return to the list and have participants ask and answer the questions on it.

Workplace Connections:

1. Ask participants to set up appointments with managers other than their own to learn the kinds of critical questions today's employees should be asking their employers and themselves.

2. Advise employees to answer the following three questions and then ask their supervisors the same questions. Once the supervisor has had an opportunity to answer the questions in reference to the employee (rather than themselves), the employee should meet with the supervisor to discuss the questions and compare the answers.

    (1) How will this job change in the next five years?

    (2) What are the five most important outputs of this job?

    (3) If I were to retire tomorrow, what qualifications would be needed by the person who replaces me?

Questions for Further Consideration:

1. Peter Drucker once observed that "…exceptional leaders know how to ask questions—the right questions." What questions do you think exceptional leaders are asking or should be asking?

2. What questions are typically asked in your staff meetings?

3. What questions would you like to have answers to?

4. What is the most difficult question you have ever been asked, and how did you respond to it?

5. What is the most difficult question you have ever asked? How was it answered?

6. What questions have you asked that led directly to the solution of a problem?

Questions Employees Are Often Asked

1. What would you do if you were in charge of this organization?

2. How can we serve our customers better?

3. What do you like best about your work?

4. How could teamwork be improved?

5. What can managers do to foster creativity?

6. What benchmarking have you done in the last six months?

7. In what ways have you demonstrated leadership?

8. What does the perfect workplace look like?

9. How can stress in the workplace be reduced?

10. How can we prepare for the future?

11. What are we doing that we shouldn't be doing?

12. What are we not doing that we should be doing?

13. How do you juggle multiple priorities?

14. How can we become one of the "world-class" competitors?

15. What is your philosophy regarding work?

16. How can we serve our community better?

17. How can we deepen our trust within the company?

18. How can we improve our communication processes?

19. What decision-making style do you admire?

20. How are problems typically solved in your work unit?

21. What is being done to ensure quality in the goods/services you provide?

22. Would you want a promotion? Why or why not?

23. What workplace myths have you encountered?

Overview:	In a recent *Forbes* magazine article written by Nina Munk and Suzanne Oliver ("Think Fast!" March 24, 1997, page 146), the authors assert, "To gauge an applicant's ability to think quickly and creatively, employers now routinely ask mind-bending brainteasers." The ability to think fast, innovatively, and logically as needed—in other words, the ability to think critically—is a prized commodity in the business world today. This activity is designed to strengthen that ability.
Objective:	To develop confidence in every participant's ability to answer questions easily and articulately.
Supplies:	Have paper and pencils available in case they are needed.
Time:	About 20 minutes
Advance Preparation:	If possible, arrange seating so teams of four can work together.
Participants/ Application:	This exercise is an adaptable one. It could be used to kick off a session, giving participants an opportunity to get to know one another. It can be used as a filler when there are spare moments before or after a break. It could also be used to reinforce instructional elements by having participants write questions related to the concepts presented.

Introduction to Concept:

It is not just in job interviews that we are asked questions that make us wonder where the question (and sometimes even the *questioner*) is coming from. Consider this real-world occurrence: A young woman in a large aerospace firm in Southern California was once asked by her boss if she thought she was intelligent. Even though the question came out of the blue, she answered in the affirmative. The next question was even more suspect: "How do you *know* you're intelligent?"

Not having been to college, the young woman was unable to point to academic credentials as proof of her intelligence. But she came up with a response (thanks to her quick-wittedness) that more than sufficed. "To me," she replied, "intelligence is knowledge. And I know more today than I knew yesterday."

Some questions send up red flags (there are people who try to set up other people), and even those questions that seem abnormal but are asked for normal reasons can throw us off guard if we have not had practice fielding them. Such questions may come from bosses, co-workers, customers, friends, spouses, strangers, even from our children. And, of course, such questions may come from interviewers (like the one who asked applicants, "How do you feel about bedbugs?" just to see if they could think on their feet).

Examples:

Interviewers generally like to ask atypical questions. For example, Bob Dylan was once asked by reporter Scott Cohen:

> What are some questions you can't answer?
> What are two truths that aren't true?
> What is the furthest thing from your mind?

The Wallace family, in their *Book of Lists,* ask such things as "What films would you recommend to insomniacs?" and "What are the most under-reported stories?" Whether or not you are well-enough known to be interviewed for publication, you are well-enough known to be asked some unusual questions by friends, family, and associates. The more experience you have in devising quick and witty answers, the more prepared you will be for the next questionable question.

Procedure:

1. Ask each participant to (neatly) write five unusual questions on each of two sheets of paper (a total of ten questions). Collect the two sets of questions from each participant and shuffle them.

2. Divide the class into teams of four. (If one, two, or three members remain, they can serve as observers in the first round, with each person sitting in on a different team.) Give one person on each team a set of five questions and another person on each team another set of five questions. While the two members with questions ask them of one another, the other members of the teams will make notes regarding what worked and what didn't work in terms of quick-witted responses.

3. When the first round is complete, give two more people on each team a set of questions each. As they ask them of one another, the remaining members of the group will again make notes about which responses/techniques proved to be effective.

4. After ten or fifteen minutes, ask one member of each team to share with the class as a whole the team notes regarding effective response tactics.

Extending the Activity:

1. Invite a reporter from the local newspaper to speak with participants about the interview process.

2. Then have participants interview interesting people in their organization or in other organizations.

3. Invite someone from the Human Resources department of a large corporation to discuss how one can best present him- or herself.

4. Ask the personnel representative to actually interview some of the class members and videotape the process.

5. Invite a representative from a different corporation to critique the participants' interviews and identify which actions/responses were most effective from their perspective.

Workplace Connections:

1. Suggest that participants team up [engage in "the buddy system"] when they return to work, with one person gathering questions based on the week's current events, and the other person answering the questions. (This technique also fosters "external awareness," a prized asset for those in leadership positions.) The next week, the two should switch positions.

2. Encourage those seeking career advancement to meet with people who currently hold positions they themselves would one day like to hold. They should have a set of 10 to 15 questions, and should give the list to the individual a week before the meeting, along with several ways to answer the questions. While participants would no doubt derive the most benefit from a face-to-face meeting, the interviewee might find it difficult to fit it into his or her schedule. So, an e-mail, telephone, or faxed response to the questions might be a better avenue for obtaining answers.

Questions for Further Consideration:

1. What are some of the toughest questions you have ever been asked?

2. What are the various types of questions that can be asked?

3. In terms of developing cognitive skills, what kinds of questions require you to think most critically?

4. In terms of problem-solving, what kinds of questions should be asked before the problem is actually tackled?

5. In terms of teams, what questions should be asked the very first time the team meets?

Overview:	With this activity, participants are given an acronymic tool for organizing their thoughts quickly and coherently.
Objective:	To use a structure that forces cogent and quick thinking in response to a given verbal stimulus.
Supplies:	• Transparency #5-1 • Overhead projector
Time:	At least 15 minutes. (The exercise may require considerably more time, depending on the size of the class and the number of participants who opt to read their work aloud.)
Advance Preparation:	Download Transparency #5-1. If possible, have a podium in the room for participants who may choose to deliver their K-W-I-C composition aloud.
Participants/ Application:	This exercise works well as a session-stimulator. Before or after delivering an instructional chunk, you may wish to generate discussion about the points you will make or have made. The feedback you will receive in the K-W-I-C replies will provide excellent discussion points for debriefing. The activity can also be used at the beginning of a session as an icebreaker, or at the end as a summarizing tool. Ideally, the class size will not exceed 20.

Introduction to Concept:

When we are asked to compose our thoughts but are not given sufficient time in which to do so, we sometimes feel mentally paralyzed. This exercise is designed to defrost brain cells that become instantaneously frozen in such circumstances. It is effective in spoken (impromptu speech) and written (examination question) situations. It also works well when you are pressured by time and must compose a letter or memo, for example, within a five- or ten-minute period.

Example:

The next time you find yourself in a "crunch" and need to prepare cogent remarks but have insufficient time in which to do so, don't panic. Just think: K-W-I-C. The **"K"** stands for the "kernel" of your remarks, the gist of your presentation, the essence or main point or purpose. It is stated succinctly. You will "widen" that basic thrust in the second or **"W"** step. Expound a bit on the purpose and broaden or expand upon the main point contained in your introductory kernel. Next, the **"I"** emphasizes the need to "illustrate" the kernel and its widened perspective. In this third stage, you will give examples and/or specific details to support the main point. In the final step, the **"C"** stands for "concluding" your remarks with a neat summary of the contents.

K—*Kernal*	Today, I would like to speak to you about our attitudes toward the abundance we have in this country.
W—*Widen*	Whether or not you call yourself a "recycler," you should be concerned about our wasteful ways.
I—*Illustrate*	Every day, American households are wasting food—32% of the vegetables we buy, for example, wind up being thrown out. The total annual waste of solid food in America would be enough to feed the entire population of Canada for one full year.
C—*Conclude*	Therefore, I ask you to join me in doing what you can to protect our precious resources. At the very least, buy only what you need. In an all-you-can-eat restaurant, take only what you can eat. For one whole day or one whole week, buy nothing for yourself. Remember, nothing says "greed" like excess!

Procedure:

1. Participants will work individually on this assignment, which begins with Transparency #5-1.

2. Throw out a topic and allow only ten minutes for them to prepare a written or spoken essay in response to your topic. (Sample subjects should relate to the nature of the training being provided. However, general business topics will serve as well: Productivity, Employee Morale, Quality, Time Management, Communication, Leadership, Innovation, Technology, Strategic Planning, etc.)

3. After ten minutes, collect the written essays and scan through them to see if participants have followed the K-W-I-C structure. Have the participants who chose the spoken essay stand and deliver their K-W-I-C responses.

Extending the Activity:

1. Turn the tables: Have participants prepare topics to be addressed by you or another instructor. Your responses, of course, must illustrate the K-W-I-C technique.

2. Give a K-W-I-C assignment periodically as the training progresses.

Workplace Connections:

1. Share with participants the fact that it takes 28 repetitions before a new skill becomes part of our behavioral repertoire. Ask each person to keep track, once the class is concluded, of the number of times he or she has employed the K-W-I-C technique. On the 28th use, the participant can e-mail you or a colleague and, hopefully, receive a congratulatory message.

2. If possible, share the K-W-I-C technique with department heads and other managers (especially the supervisors of those in attendance) and encourage its use department-wide.

Questions for Further Consideration:

1. What other communication shortcuts do you use?

2. What impression is created by those who ramble?

3. How can you help those inclined to show you how a watch is made when all you asked for was the time?

4. How much time do you typically take to write a business memo?

5. How much time will it take by using the K-W-I-C model?

K = **Kernel**

W = **Widen**

I = **Illustrate**

C = **Conclude**

Overview:	This activity asks participants to think quickly and logically when given seemingly disparate bits of information. The ability to synthesize, to make connections, to discern relationships not readily apparent is an integral element of critical thinking.
Objective:	To give participants a chance to practice seeing relationships and making associations within a limited period of time.
Supplies:	• Copies of Handout #6-1, cut into strips • 3" x 5" cards (three for each participant) • Flipchart (optional)
Time:	Approximately 15 minutes
Advance Preparation:	Make copies of Handout #6-1 (one-third the actual number of participants, as the handout can be cut into three strips). If possible, arrange participants in table groups of four.
Participants/ Application:	This exercise, which can be used with any size group, is flexible enough to use at any time during the training day. It serves equally well as a warm-up, as a session-stimulator, and as a summarizing activity (with the stipulation that the remarks would have to serve as concluding statements).

Introduction to Concept:

Babies have populated the earth since man (and woman, of course) first appeared on it. Vegetables have probably been around just as long. Not until the 1980s, however, has a photographer decided to put the two together. In so doing, Anne Geddes created an empire and has been crowned, however unintentionally, its empress.

When we juxtapose seemingly unrelated entities, we create the unexpected. To develop the skill of being able to move fluidly between two elements and make connections between things that seem to have no connection at all, you only need to practice.

Procedure:

1. Ask participants to jot down on a sheet of scrap paper the first word that comes into their heads. Call on two people at random and, using their two words, make a short essay presentation that relates to the program being presented. For example, if the two words were "tired" and "behind," you might connect them with a monologue like the following:

    I know how demanding your jobs are—some of you are probably doing the work of one-and-a-half or even two people. Many of us probably came to this training session today quite tired, *worried about the work that continues to pile up on our desks, even when we are not there. Such concern is normal. In fact, it bespeaks your conscientious nature. Why? Because if you are thinking about work, you are not thinking about the training. And you are being paid today—not to work, but to learn. Secondly, you will always be* behind. *In fact, I used to work for a supervisor who told me, "The day you find yourself all caught up is the day I fire you." The average American employee has 37 hours' worth of untouched work sitting on his or her desk on any given day. So... knowing that the work you have to do will always be there, and knowing that you are expected to acquire knowledge today, I invite you to sit back, take notes, participate, and absorb as much as you can.*

It is important to begin talking as quickly as possible, for this exercise calls upon all three of the elements comprising critical thought: speed, creativity, and logic. (If you should flub your chance, use your less-than-perfect performance to illustrate [1] how difficult it is to engage in this kind of thinking; [2] that more practice brings us closer to the ideal; and [3] that participants can do no worse than you have done.)

2. Distribute three 3" x 5" cards to each person in the four-person groups. Explain that each member will evaluate each of the other members' presentations using a number from 1 (low) to 10 (high) to evaluate the presentations made in the small group. After each presentation, the three evaluators will fold their cards in half and present them to the speaker, who will average the scores.

3. Distribute the handout strips. Ask each person to select one pair and make as creative and logical a mini-speech as they can, making certain to use the two words as the basis of their presentation. While the first person is speaking, the others should be listening—not looking at their handouts and/or preparing their own remarks. (You may choose to give a handout to each team member just before he or she speaks in order to prevent advance preparation.)

4. Determine who has the highest score(s). Ask that person(s) to come forward and repeat their stellar performance(s) if they are willing to do so.

Extending the Activity:

1. Make another sheet of juxtaposed pairs. This one, however, should include words that have some relationship (albeit not too obvious a connection) to the material being studied. Conduct the procedure in the same way.

2. Call aside one member of the class at the very beginning of the training session. Ask him or her to make a list of words equaling twice the number of participants as the class proceeds. (If there are 15 attendees, for example, the person making the list would need to have 30 words.) The words should be ones that come up frequently during class discussions, or words the list-maker finds interesting in relation to the class, or perhaps words that were not understood by class members, or words the facilitator uses frequently.

    At the first break (or during lunch), write the words on a flip chart. Then, in the afternoon session, periodically call upon a participant to choose two words from the list and unite them in a logical fashion. When he or she finishes, cross off the words so the next person will not repeat them.

Workplace Connections:

1. Ask for volunteers to make a brief presentation at the next training session. As they address participants at the beginning of the next class, the volunteers will use as their prepared remarks a refined version of the extended activity.

2. Ask those who seemed to especially enjoy this activity if they would be willing to prepare a signed one-page (maximum) statement about the course that you can distribute to future participants.

Questions for Further Consideration:

1. When was the last time you were at a loss for words?

2. What impressions do others form of us when we are unable to articulate our thoughts easily?

3. Initially confusing input, rescued by critical thinking, often yields significant outputs. Can you think of a time when you were presented with ideas or situations that caused chaos at first, but ultimately resulted in valued insights?

movie – business card	mouse – dial	witch – staple	judge – parade
cellophane – squirrel	tape – alliance	brick – curl	pill – glasses
modem – vitality	caterpillar – bat	rainbow – pool	cloud – modem
gem – leadership	nail – chord	cholesterol – clerk	focus – barn
calendar – grape	money – stray	phobia – e-mail	clock – worm
Olympics – grass	flower – conflict	sponge – cycle time	persuasion – wing
résumé – sleeve	criticism – attitude	diversity – yo-yo	culture – change
violin – supervision	nature – computer	customer – frog	discipline – interviews
football – appraisal	teamwork – peacock	lawsuit – scissors	surgery – diplomacy

movie – business card	mouse – dial	witch – staple	judge – parade
cellophane – squirrel	tape – alliance	brick – curl	pill – glasses
modem – vitality	caterpillar – bat	rainbow – pool	cloud – modem
gem – leadership	nail – chord	cholesterol – clerk	focus – barn
calendar – grape	money – stray	phobia – e-mail	clock – worm
Olympics – grass	flower – conflict	sponge – cycle time	persuasion – wing
résumé – sleeve	criticism – attitude	diversity – yo-yo	culture – change
violin – supervision	nature – computer	customer – frog	discipline – interviews
football – appraisal	teamwork – peacock	lawsuit – scissors	surgery – diplomacy

movie – business card	mouse – dial	witch – staple	judge – parade
cellophane – squirrel	tape – alliance	brick – curl	pill – glasses
modem – vitality	caterpillar – bat	rainbow – pool	cloud – modem
gem – leadership	nail – chord	cholesterol – clerk	focus – barn
calendar – grape	money – stray	phobia – e-mail	clock – worm
Olympics – grass	flower – conflict	sponge – cycle time	persuasion – wing
résumé – sleeve	criticism – attitude	diversity – yo-yo	culture – change
violin – supervision	nature – computer	customer – frog	discipline – interviews
football – appraisal	teamwork – peacock	lawsuit – scissors	surgery – diplomacy

Overview: When we are asked to generate detailed information within a particular time-frame, we call upon a special kind of intelligence. This intelligence permits us to filter all we know through the sieve of specificity in order to isolate information that conforms to the criteria we have been issued. This activity asks participants to respond quickly but appropriately to the matrix provided.

Objective: To present participants with the opportunity to generate specific data in response to given prompts.

Supplies: Transparency #7-1
Timer

Time: 25 minutes

Participants/ Application: Whenever you sense that the energy level is dropping among participants, you can use this exercise. It is a quick means of recapping the major concepts thus far presented. It begins with a warm-up, which works especially well when participants are seated in table groups of five to eight participants. From there, participants work a second time to generate as many ideas as possible within time limits.

Introduction to Concept:

On exhibit at the John F. Kennedy Memorial Library are notes written in the President's hand, reflecting his interest in skill-building activities of the cerebral type. These brainbusters challenge and entertain us, develop our concentrative abilities, and sharpen our wits.

Procedure:

1. Use the following set of directions for the three warm-up activities.

   Today we are going to work on one brainbuster the way President Kennedy used to do. To prepare ourselves for the Presidential pastime, we will first do a few warm-ups. I'm going to set the timer now for three minutes. During that time, you and the other members of your table group will make as long a list as possible of words that are spelled with three letters only—words that refer to our physical essence. The words cannot end in "s" and you should know that there are more than 30 of them, such as "arm" or "eye." *[After three minutes…]*

   Next, I'm going to give you another three minutes. This time, you will create as long a list as possible of words with four letters that refer to our physical essence. The words cannot end in "s" and you should know that there are more than 30 of them, such as "face" or "neck." *[After three minutes…]*

   Now, I'm going to set the timer for another three minutes. You will work in your group to list as many words as you can referring to our physical essence. The words must be nouns and must be spelled with five letters, such as "elbow" or "femur." As you may have guessed, the words cannot end in "s."

Repeat the process two additional times. In the fourth round, the words must have six letters, such as "muscle" or "tendon." In the fifth round, the words must have seven, such as "eardrum" or "stomach."

2. After completing the warm-up activities (and determining each time which group had the longest lists), go over their answers.

Extending the Activity:

1. Use transparency 7-1 to make up a matrix related to the topic of the course. Using any combination of letters across the top, write in the vertical column words pertinent to the course. If it is a course in supervision, for example, the words in the left column might be People, Processes, Profits, Quality, Customers, and Communications. Taking the first word, People, across the horizontal columns, you might have Productivity, Development, Filing, Authority, and Motivation.

2. Call upon individuals or teams periodically throughout the training program to complete challenges like the following within a specified period of time:

   a. List ten ways to motivate employees without spending more than ten dollars.
   b. List ten ways empowerment benefits individuals, teams, and/or the organization.
   c. List fifteen ways of managing stress in the workplace.

3. There are also more than 30 words with eight letters, such as "clavicle," should you choose to assign the task of listing them.

Procedure:

1. Encourage participants to put idle moments to work by keeping matrixes like this by the phone (for use whenever they are "on hold"). As soon as one has been completed, they can begin the next. The matrixes, again, can be any combination of letters and any combination of categories: Geographic Locations, Musical Instruments, or Pieces of Equipment, for example.

2. Speak with the editor of the company newsletter about holding a monthly contest with organization-specific categories for the matrix.

Questions for Further Consideration:

1. Can you think of a time when your ability to think and/or act quickly proved to be critically important?

2. As you think about your own profession, what trends do you see emerging?

3. What percentage of your reading is totally unrelated to the work you do? (Experts tell us it should be 35%.)

4. What connections can you make between what you do in your life outside work and what you do when you are at work?

5. How do you use spare moments productively?

6. Who is the most efficient/busiest person you know? How does he or she manage to get so much done?

Supervision

	P	*D*	*F*	*A*	*M*
People					
Processes					
Profits					
Quality					
Customers					
Communications					

Overview: Those whose mouths are wide enough to accommodate their frequently inserted feet have not practiced the skill of saying the *second* thing that comes to mind. This activity will assist participants to think fluidly, critically assess a situation, and then translate thought into words most appropriate for the circumstances.

Objective: To instill confidence in participants' ability to think before they speak.

Supplies:
- 3" x 5" cards
- Transparency #8-1
- Overhead projector
- Flipchart

Time: Approximately 20 minutes

Advance Preparation: Download Transparency #8-1. If possible, arrange seating flexibly, as participants will first work in pairs, then in teams of four, then in teams of six, and finally in teams of eight. (Exact numbers are not important because leftover participants can easily fit into any existing team.)

Prepare the 3" x 5" cards by writing one of the following sentences on each of 15 cards. (If the class has more than 30 participants, write additional sentences—one for every two participants.)

- Tell someone you think he or she should not be reading novels during working hours.
- Tell someone you think he or she does not dress appropriately.
- Tell someone you think he or she spends too much time on the phone making personal calls.
- Tell someone you think he or she flirts too much.
- Tell someone you think he or she is not doing enough work.
- Tell someone you think he or she is not a team player.
- Tell someone you think he or she should not bring personal problems into the office.
- Tell someone you think he or she should not smoke.
- Tell someone you think he or she should not make sexist remarks.
- Tell someone you think he or she has an ageism bias.
- Tell someone you think his or her work area is too messy.
- Tell someone you think he or she should not have so many stuffed animals in his or her office.
- Tell someone you think he or she shows favoritism.
- Tell someone you think he or she needs to take additional training in a particular area.
- Tell someone you think he or she gossips too much

Participants/ Application: This exercise works best with small groups. Ideally, participants will have had a chance to work together before engaging in it, for some might feel initially awkward with the difficult messages they are expected to deliver. In terms of sequence, the exercise works well after a large or complicated instructional segment has been presented.

Introduction to Concept:

Only if we own and operate our own one-man or one-woman business do we have the arguable "luxury" of keeping our own company. Even then, we must work with vendors and clients. And so, as you are developing expertise today in [mention name of course], keep in mind that such expertise will not be fully appreciated if you are unable to work well with others. This activity will develop your ability to say what needs to be said in the most diplomatic and non-offensive way possible.

Procedure:

1. Divide the group into pairs. If one person is left over, he or she can serve as your partner or can serve as a roving observer. Explain that one person in the pair will have a difficult message to deliver, written on a 3" x 5" card. That person will be asked to deliver the message as honestly but as kindly as possible. The partner— acknowledging that this is a classroom exercise, not real life—promises not to become enraged, but to instead respond in a way that will defuse a potentially explosive situation.

    This may mean that the partner must force him- or herself to say the second thing that comes into his or her head. For example, if I were told by a friend or co-worker that he or she thought I had a drinking problem, my first reaction might be, "What business is it of yours, you jerk?" That is not the response I would give, however, unless I wanted to cut off discussion then and there. A reply such as, "What makes you say that, Tom?" would lead to better understanding between the parties involved.

2. Ask one person in each pair to select one card and deliver the message on the card in as supportive a manner as possible. Once the message has been delivered, the recipient is asked to reply in a non-confrontational manner, weighing his or her words carefully before expressing them.

3. After the first exchange, have the pairs quietly discuss with one another their responses t o the questions on the transparency. Allow five minutes for this. [Show transparency now.]

4. Collect and shuffle the 3" x 5" cards. Ask the pairs to join with other pairs so foursomes are created.

5. Ask one person in each foursome to select a card and confer with his or her original partner to figure out the best way to deliver the news. (If you wish to keep the other pair engaged while the first discussion is going on, use a warm-up.)

6. After a few moments, one member of the card-bearing pair will express the sentiment on the card to the other pair. The second pair can respond in singular or tandem fashion. Afterwards, ask the foursome to discuss their reactions to the assignment. For example, did the message-deliverers feel a bit more confident/comfortable the second time around? Did the message-receivers find themselves reacting less emotionally than they did the first time?

7. Collect the cards and ask each foursome to join another foursome. A team of four will next select one card and discuss the most professional/gracious way to deliver the message it contains. (Again, while they wait, the other team could work on a mind-bending exercise such as: "Make a list as long as you possibly can of titles (book, movies, opera, ballet, song, poem) that contain a geographic allusion, such as 'The Barber of Seville.'")

8. Once the foursome has had a few moments to prepare, a spokesperson from the group will deliver the message. One person from the other foursome will react to it.

9. Lead a discussion with the class as a whole to learn if participants feel they are becoming more skilled with each successive exercise. Make certain to call on one person from each foursome to share specific techniques or phrases that worked well, and record these on the flipchart as they are being shared.

Extending the Activity:

1. In the week prior to the class you are scheduled to facilitate, collect examples from the daily newspaper of arguments or controversy that ensued over issues that were not well-communicated. Use these as the basis for class discussions.

2. Divide the class into small groups and give this assignment: Assume that you were asked to develop an outline for a class to be titled, "Making the hard-to-swallow easy-to-digest." How would you design the curriculum?

Workplace Connections:

1. Suggest that participants keep a journal listing potentially volatile workplace issues and how they were handled. Each entry should be followed by a description of how the journal-keeper would have handled the situation.

2. Ask for volunteers to form a focus group that will meet with the Personnel or Human Resources Department to discuss ways of reducing or preventing workplace conflicts.

Questions for Further Consideration:

1. Have you ever been in a situation that required you to say something you feared might hurt the other person's feelings? If so, how did you handle it?

2. Think of times when other people shared similar information with you. How did they handle it?

3. Considering your own experiences with supervisors/managers, were they skilled in presenting unwelcome information in a positive way? Explain.

1. *How did you feel as your partner told you what he or she thought?*

2. *Do you think he or she expressed his or her thoughts diplomatically?*

3. *Were you able to hold your tongue as you listened? Explain how you did or didn't do this.*

4. *What were you thinking as you listened to your partner?*

5. *What did you actually say in response to what you heard?*

6. *What would you do differently the next time?*

Overview:	Brainteasers for some represent a competitive (sometimes self-competitive) challenge. When brainteasers are used in hiring situations however, with the prospective employer timing the candidate's response time, we may feel our brain is being squeezed rather than teased. This activity gives participants a chance to make educated guesses or calculated answers to various questions—some of which are actually part of interview situations.
Objective:	To enable participants to estimate numerical answers more accurately.
Supplies:	• Copies of Worksheet #9-1 • Copies of Handout #9-1 (optional)
Time:	20 minutes
Advance Preparation:	Make copies of Worksheet #9-1 (and Handout #9-1 if using the extending activity), one for each participant.
Participants/ Application:	This exercise works well as an icebreaker, in which case you would ask small groups to work together. It also works as a post-break segue to the "mind-bending" material you plan to present in the next instructional segment. Any number of participants can be involved.

Introduction to Concept:

The interview process has changed, as has every other process in the world of business. No longer are applicants asked only comforting and comfortable questions, such as "Tell me about yourself." To be considered for a position in today's demanding workplace, job candidates are often asked demanding questions. At first, some questions may seem impossible to answer. As our brains kick into gear and as we begin to critically assess the problem statement, we find we can approximate if not accurately figure an answer.

Example:

A recent *Forbes* article reported that McKinsey and Company, a Chicago consulting firm, asks job applicants, "How many barbers are there in Chicago?" Your private, initial reaction most likely is, "I have no idea. And if I am expected to know trivia like this, then I don't want to work here." However, there's a method in the seeming madness here. Such questions permit others to assess your analytical skills as well as your ability to think well and quickly when under pressure.

Does anyone have any ideas on how to figure out this problem? (Elicit discussion before continuing.) In fact, you can guesstimate the answer. (After presenting each of the steps supplied in the *Forbes* article, lead a short discussion, asking participants how they would use this knowledge. What would they do next?)

1. Begin with the population of the city, 2.7 million. (If you lived in Chicago, you'd probably know this. If not, ask the interviewer to tell you.)

2. Assume half the population, 1.35 million, is male.

3. Assume every boy or man has his hair cut once every two months or six times a year.

4. Multiply 6 times 1.35 million and you get 8.1 million haircuts a year.

5. Determine how many haircuts the average barber can give a day—probably one every half hour or 15 in a workday of seven and one-half hours.

6. Assume that the average barber works six days a week. This means he (or she) does 90 haircuts a week, or 4,680 a year.

7. Divide 8.1 million by 4,680 to learn the number of barbers needed; 1,730 will be your answer.

With such questions, prospective employers are not looking for the right answer. They are looking for critical thinking skills that employ logic and rapidity in breaking a problem down and following a sequential process to solve it. Individuals who can operate in such a way evince—both intellectually and psychologically—an undaunted approach.

Procedure:

1. Distribute the worksheet. Tell participants to work alone or with one or several other persons—whatever they are most comfortable with. However, if they work with others, they should talk in whispers so other participants are not distracted. (If a breakout room is available, have those who wish to work together work there.)

2. After ten minutes, share the answers:

    1) We have in this situation three men: Jim, Dave, and Paul. We know Dave is the married man. We also know that Jim is not the bachelor, so it must be Paul who is. He has the same color eyes as Jim. Therefore, Paul and Jim have blue eyes. This leaves Dave with brown eyes and a beard.

    2) Denise did not go to Tulsa or Boston, so she went to Skokie. Harriette did not go to Tulsa, so she went to Boston. Therefore, the third person went to Tulsa.

    3) More. The second fish weighs twenty pounds, as shown in the following equation:

$$W = 10 + \tfrac{1}{2}W$$
$$W - \tfrac{1}{2}W = 10$$
$$\tfrac{1}{2}W = 10$$
$$W = 20$$

4)

4	9	2
3	5	7
8	1	6

5) 40, found by working backwards. Choose an answer and see if it works. In this case, half of 40 is 20, and 20 minus 5 is 15. 15/40 is the same as 3/8.

Extending the Activity:

1. A less stressful exercise asks each participant to figure out the age of their partner. (Because some people may be sensitive about revealing their age, assure all that they need not give the exact age to their questioner, but rather simply need to tell which column(s) contains their age out of a list of 32 numbers. Or suggest that they be given the worksheet to figure out their partner's age.) Divide the class into pairs and distribute Handout #9-1 to half the participants and ask them to figure out the age of their partner. Once they have done so, give a copy of the handout to the partners so they can use the age-determiner with their own colleagues.

Workplace Connections:

1. Suggest that a team of participants contact the Personnel or Human Resources Department after completing the training program to learn what types of questions are actually presented to candidates for various positions. They can gain quick-thinking practice by answering these questions with a colleague.

2. Encourage employees to ask their supervisors what answers (to which questions) would be most valued by the supervisor. Comparisons could then be made to the answers participants actually gave to their colleagues.

3. Ask for volunteers to organize a Monthly Mindbender or Corporate Conundrum contest. The first person to contact a committee member with the correct answer could be awarded a token prize and recognized in some public way within the company.

Questions for Further Consideration:

1. What was your first reaction to the barber question?

2. Once you saw how the approximate answer was derived, did you realize that you could have followed those steps fairly easily?

3. Exactly what prevented you from figuring out the barber problem? (Lack of knowledge, lack of confidence, lack of linear-thinking skills, lack of math ability, lack of time, lack of a calculator?) If you were able to determine how the problem could be solved, exactly what led you to the correct process?

4. What is gained, in your opinion, from asking such questions during the interview process?

5. What might be lost because such questions are asked?

Directions: You have an average of two minutes to solve each problem. If you finish ahead of the others, please work quietly on the brainteaser that appears at the bottom of this page. (Or go back and check your work, as accuracy is as important as speed, and more important in some cases.)

1. At the annual industry trade show, technocrats had an opportunity to network and learn about the latest technology. Marya was telling LaTeisha that she had met a bearded man from a competing firm but she wasn't certain if he was married. LaTeisha, who knew all three of the men from the firm, decided to challenge Marya's brain. "I know who he is," she declared. "Now you figure this out. Two of them are married, two have blue eyes, and two are clean-shaven. The one with the beard has brown eyes. Dave's wife is Paul's sister, and the bachelor is the one with the same color eyes Jim has." Which man has the beard?

2. Three managers were sent on business trips but did not go together. One went to Tulsa, one went to Skokie, and one went to Boston. Harriette will be going to Tulsa for the first time next December. Denise has refused to go to Tulsa because of an unpleasant incident that occurred the last time she was there. Because she is an excellent employee, her boss has also granted her wish not to go to Boston, where her ex-husband lives. What city was each manager in?

3. Two colleagues went on a fishing trip together. Always competitive in sales, they were equally competitive in their sports pursuits. The first man caught a fish that weighed 18 pounds. The fish the second man caught weighed ten pounds plus half of its weight. Did the second man's fish weigh more or less than the first man's?

4. Arrange the numbers from 1 to 9 so that the total is 15 when three numbers are added either horizontally, vertically, or diagonally.

5. At a well-attended ice skating exhibition, the cotton candy vendor sold half her candy before the intermission. By the end of the next skater's performance, she had sold five more cotton candy cones, leaving her with three-eighths of the original number of cones. How many cotton candy cones did she have to sell when she started?

   a) 10   b) 20   c) 30   d) 40   e) 50   f) 60   g) Other

Brainteaser for those who finish early: On the back of this paper, make as long a list as you possibly can of titles (book, poem, movie, song, opera, ballet, television programs, and so on) that contain a month or season reference, such as "April in Paris."

Directions: Show these six columns to your partner and ask him or her to tell you which columns his or her age appears in. Then, all you have to do is add the top number in each of those columns containing the age. The total of the top numbers in columns containing the age will equal the person's age. Fold at the dotted line before showing the columns.

1	2	4	8	16	32
3	3	5	9	17	33
5	6	6	10	18	34
7	7	7	11	19	35
9	10	12	12	20	36
11	11	13	13	21	37
13	14	14	14	22	38
15	15	15	15	23	39
17	18	20	24	24	40
19	19	21	25	25	41
21	22	22	26	26	42
23	23	23	26	26	43
25	26	28	28	28	44
27	27	29	29	29	45
29	30	30	30	30	46
31	31	31	31	31	47
33	34	36	40	48	48
35	35	37	41	49	49
37	38	38	42	50	50
39	39	39	43	51	51
41	42	44	44	52	52
43	43	45	45	53	53
45	46	46	46	54	54
47	47	47	47	55	55
49	50	52	56	56	56
51	51	53	57	57	57
53	54	54	58	58	58
55	55	55	59	59	59
57	58	60	60	60	60
59	59	61	61	61	61
61	62	62	62	62	63
63	63	63	63	63	63

Overview:	Two short but challenging activities are presented here. Each is designed to heighten sensitivity to the separate structural elements of a situation, whether a single word is involved or a workplace problem.
Objective:	To encourage the development of multiple perspectives from which a given situation or problem can be viewed.
Supplies:	• Transparencies #10-1 and #10-2 • Overhead projector • Copies of Worksheet #10-1
Time:	10–15 minutes
Advance Preparation:	Download Transparency #10-1 and Transparency #10-2. Make copies of Handout #10-1 (one for each participant).
Participants/ Application:	This mind-bending exercise can be used at any time during the course of the training program by any number of participants who can work alone, in pairs, triads, or in small table groups.

Introduction to Concept:

Optical illusions allow our eyes to play tricks on us. We seem to have a fixed perceptual view, but when a slight shift occurs that perceptual view becomes another, often quite different, view. The reality remains the same, but somehow, our perception of that reality undergoes a transformation. In terms of our attitudes, our core values remain constant, and well they should. Other attitudes need to be periodically updated or calibrated to reflect the growth we are experiencing in the course of living. "A foolish consistency," as Emerson pointed out, "is the hobgoblin of little minds."

Example:

I am going to show you part of a word that you know very well. I have removed three letters from the front of the word and three letters from the end of the word. (Show Transparency #10-1.) The three letters removed in the beginning are the same three letters removed from the end. Can you figure out the word? (Allow just a few moments for this, as it is extremely difficult to recognize the word "underground" when the "und" parts of it are gone.)

Procedure:

1. Begin by showing the old woman/young woman drawing on Transparency #10-2. Discuss the features that can be seen in each in order to help participants see both.

2. Ask participants how they would like to work (alone, in pairs, in small groups) and distribute Worksheet #10-1 accordingly. Encourage them to work as quickly as they do on intelligence and entrance exams, which test for both accuracy and speed.

3. After ten minutes, share the answers, which are:

1. art	9. ink
2. ate	10. ire
3. one	11. and
4. end	12. eat
5. at	13. eight
6. are	14. eel
7. own	15. ill
8. ear	16. ace

Extending the Activity:

1. Take familiar words that relate directly to the training you are facilitating and write them with parts of the words missing. In a class on workplace violence, for example, the word "c-o-n-f-l-i-c-t" might be written as _ _ nfl _ _ _. When you have ten or twenty words, write them on the flipchart and have participants figure them out.

2. Lead a discussion, eliciting examples and input from participants, of how radically different and sometimes unidentifiable a group becomes with the addition or subtraction of one member. Point out that when we work cohesively, as an integrated unit, things are as they should be. But when we allow factions and fractious behavior to exist, work units disintegrate; they turn into something that is often unrecognizable as productive behavior. Have a recorder list the ways synergy can be developed in the workplace.

Workplace Connections:

1. Ask for a volunteer to prepare a survey, with questions related to employees' feelings about various issues relevant to either organizational thrusts or to instructional emphasis. Have this person distribute the survey once it has been approved and again six months later. He or she can compare the results to learn if attitudinal shifts have occurred, and can then report the data-analysis in an approved format.

2. Suggest that an informal committee be formed to compare mission statements, orientation information, annual reports, and the like from the year the organization was founded to the present. Have the committee analyze what has remained the same, what has shifted somewhat, and what has undergone radical transformations.

Questions for Further Consideration:

1. What values have remained constants in your life since you first acquired them?

2. What values or attitudes or perspective shifts have you undergone:
   - Since high school?
   - Since entering the workforce?
   - Since you began working for your current supervisor?
   - Since you have attended training programs?

3. What do you think about people who think today exactly the way they thought ten years ago?

4. What changes in perception do you think you will have to undergo as the future becomes the present?

5. What perceptual shifts have occurred in your organization?

6. What changes in attitude have we undergone as a nation?

_ _ _ _ *ergro* _ _ _

Directions: The number of blanks in each example tells you the number of letters in each word. In the example shown, there are four blanks and the answer is the word "i-n-c-h," which has four letters. When you have the right word, it will create new words with each of the letters or letter-combinations on the left of the word. So, "inch" becomes "pinch," "flinch," "cinch," "winch," and "clinch."

Example: *P*
            FL
            C   _ _ _ _
            W
            CL

1. *ST*
    C
    D
    M   _ _ _
    P
    T
    W

2. *ST*
    F
    S   _ _ _
    L
    GR
    H

3. *G*
    ST
    T   _ _ _
    D
    PH

4. *S*
    F
    W   _ _ _
    T
    B

5. *P*
    S
    C   _ _
    R
    H
    M

6. *ST*
    C
    B   _ _ _
    D
    F
    H

7. *T*
    D
    FL   _ _ _
    SH
    CL

8. G
    R
    T   — — —
    D
    SP

9. W
    S
    BR
    TH   — — —
    ST
    L
    P
    M

10. F
    D
    M
    H   — — —
    S
    T
    ASP

11. W
    S
    L
    GR   — — —
    ST
    B
    H

12. P
    B
    S
    F
    GR   — — —
    H
    M
    N
    WH

13. W
    H   — — — — —
    SL
    FR

14. WH
    F
    P   — — —
    H
    K
    E

15. W
    B
    ST
    FR
    K
    SP
    D   — — —
    F
    G
    J
    H
    M
    P
    QU

16. GR
    P
    F
    L
    M   — — —
    C
    R
    BR
    PL

Overview:	There are two parts to this activity. Participants begin with easy, lighthearted oxymoronic expressions. Then, they are asked to amplify oxymorons in relation to the workplace, developing as they do so the awareness that the first step in learning is confusion.
Objective:	To expose participants to dialectical thought, requiring them to make sense (synthesis) of two seemingly contradictory viewpoints (thesis, antithesis).
Supplies:	• Worksheets #11-1 and #11-2 • Long table (optional)
Time:	Approximately 25 minutes
Advance Preparation:	Make copies of both worksheets, one of each per participant. If flexible seating is possible, arrange for participants to sit together in groups of four. If a long table is available, put it in the front of the room with several chairs (enough for a spokesperson from each group). The spokespersons will sit facing the other participants.
Participants/ Application:	This exercise can be used as a brainteaser at the beginning of a training session or as an energizer at any point during the program. Depending on the nature of the training being done, the organizational oxymorons can be tailored to coincide with particular instructional emphases in such areas as supervision, management, team-building, or planning and preparation for the future.

Introduction to Concept:

Harvard professor Charles Handy talks about living in an age of paradox. With life proceeding at an ever-faster, ever-more-complex pace, change is thrust upon us at an almost dizzying speed. Sometimes, it seems as if we have just acclimated ourselves to a particular way of thinking or acting when we are asked to change our thinking to accommodate new information.

A kind of cognitive dissonance is created as we struggle to cling to what makes sense. We find ourselves propelled to accept the non-sense and apparent nonsense of a whole new set of behaviors or thoughts. In a way, we are asked to hold two opposing views in our minds at the same time and walk along a mental tightrope stretched taut between those two points.

Procedure:

1. Make a transition to the more challenging half of this activity by using Worksheet #11-1. Distribute it to participants and ask them to review and discuss the items. Call upon a few people at random to explain the meaning of several of the terms.

2. Ask teams to add oxymorons of their own.

3. Call on several teams to share what they have thought of and encourage others to add these other oxymorons to their own lists.

4. Now distribute Worksheet #11-2. Ask participants to work together to:

   a. Discuss the confusion/stress/difficulty caused by these antithetical pushes.
   b. Offer suggestions for coping with the conflict and finding syntheses that can serve as compromises.
   c. Explain the organizational oxymorons, either in terms of how they have come about or with examples of individuals who can satisfy the opposing demands imposed by the organizational oxymorons.

5. Ask each team to send a representative to the front of the room to serve on a panel that will discuss the confusion, suggestions, and explanations.

Extending the Activity:

1. Invite a member of senior management to address the class and give his or her opinion regarding the oxymorons presented in Worksheet #11-2.

2. Ask participants to share examples of empowerment initiatives in which they are engaged. Then ask who has the final word on decisions regarding those initiatives. Lead a discussion of whether or not existing practices contradict the concept of empowerment.

Workplace Connections:

1. Propose the creation of a video that explores the apparent contradictions employees face. If it turns out well, suggest that participants work to have it become part of employee orientation.

2. Suggest that participants speak with their supervisors about the possibility of beginning each staff meeting with a few minutes devoted to the exploration of paradoxes that may be causing distress among employees. (For those participants who are supervisors, determine how willing they would be to institute this oxymoronic beginning at staff meetings.)

Questions for Further Consideration:

1. What organizational oxymorons have you encountered in your work life?

2. What do you do to resolve the contradictions you face from time to time?

3. Supervisors still supervise. What changes have you personally witnessed or learned about?

4. What behaviors are rewarded in your organization?

5. Does the reward process coincide with or conflict with what management says we should be doing?

6. Does your organization encourage risk-taking, or playing it safe?

7. What is the corporate view concerning issues that have the paradox-potential embedded within them? For example:

   - Productivity versus work/life balance
   - Discipline versus innovation
   - Independent thinking versus fierce loyalty
   - The need for quality versus the need for a downsized workforce

The Greek prefix "oxy" means "wise" and "moron," of course, means "fool." Is it possible for a person to be a "wise fool"? Quite! Initially, the words seem to contradict themselves, but we find our language strewn with such puzzling terms. During the Watergate scandal, for example, a Congressman serving on the investigative committee actually told the press the committee had reached an "inconclusive conclusion."

Here is a list of familiar oxymoronic terms. How many can you add to the list?

non-conforming conformist	fight for peace
cruel kindness	make haste slowly
night light	light heavyweight
pretty ugly	inside out
dotted line	dry martini
bittersweet	majority of one
militant pacifist	sober drunk
stupid know-it-all	cold sweat
impossible hope	living dead
dull shine	formless shape
civil war	back side
slow speed	scheduled delay

exceptional mediocrity

peacekeeper missile

sounds of silence

same difference

_____

_____

_____

_____

_____

_____

_____

_____

Directions: The following entries may appear confusing at first, for the terms in each entry seem to contradict each other. As a team, your job (for as many entries as you can) is to:

    a.   Discuss the confusion/stress/difficulty caused by these antithetical pushes.

    b.   Offer suggestions for coping with the conflict and finding syntheses that can serve as compromises.

    c.   Explicate the organizational oxymorons, either in terms of how they have come about or with examples of individuals who can satisfy the opposing demands imposed by the organizational oxymorons.

Afterwards, select a spokesperson to serve on a panel with representatives from the other teams. Essentially, the spokespersons will share the insights created by your team.

1.   The people who never experience success in their careers are the ones who always do what they are told and the ones who never do what they are told.

2.   Certain principles sustain organizations in times of radical change. And certain principles, precisely because they have been sustained too long, have created the very difficulty that makes change imperative.

3.   Seek clarity. Accept chaos.

4.   Americans are admired for their rugged individualism. And yet, in some companies, if you are not a team player, you will not be hired.

5.   Despite a plethora of time-saving devices, we seem to have less time than ever before.

6.   We are advised to "look out for #1" and yet we respect those who put the welfare of others above (or at least equal to) their own.

7.   Managers should be "hands-on" people exhibiting a "hands-off" policy.

8.   Throughout our lives, we are encouraged to learn big words. And yet, at work, we are encouraged to follow the advice of Winston Churchill: "Big [wo]men use little words."

9.   Do it right the first time but learn from your mistakes.

Overview: First, participants will work on an activity that frequently appears on intelligence tests and entrance tests for high-intelligence organizational groups. It asks participants to find a word that is linked to three other words in each entry. Participants will then shift to an exercise that will improve their ability to spot emerging trends.

Objective: To help participants develop the ability to make associations.

Supplies:
- Worksheets #12-1 and #12-2
- Flipchart paper
- Masking tape

Time: About 25 minutes

Advance Preparation: Make enough copies of the worksheets so that each participant has a copy of each. If possible, arrange the seating to permit small groups of three or four to work together.

Participants/ Application: This exercise works with any size group. It is flexible enough to be used as an introductory warm-up, as a mid-point time of reflection, as an energizer, or as a means of wrapping up the training program (especially if the first extended activity is presented).

Introduction to Concept:

Critical thinking involves the ability to "go beyond what is given," in the words of learning theorist Jerome Bruner. As we reach for a new, higher level of understanding, we are assimilating what is given with what has already been obtained, and creating a new direction in which the new elements can logically move.

The ability to find patterns and understand how and what trends may be emerging is particularly prized when change is the order of the day. Not only can we lessen our vulnerability on a personal level by understanding what may be "coming down the pike," we can also lessen it on the professional level. The first part of this exercise has you work on stratifications. These will serve as preludes to the second task, which has you and your team members assess information and make educated prognoses based on what you are given.

Procedure:

1. Divide the class into teams of three or four.

2. Distribute Worksheet #12-1 and ask teams to collaborate on the answers. After ten minutes, share these with them: 1–dog, 2–make, 3–down, 4–wear, 5–night, 6–crust, 7–paper, 8–house, 9–ball, 10–escape, 11–bowl, 12–cat, 13–pot, 14–pea, 15–road, 16–wheel, 17–shot, 18–neck, 19–phone, 20–book. (If any one person or team finishes with remarkable speed, ask them to share the secrets behind their quick-thinking skills.)

3. Distribute Worksheet #12-2. Allow about 15 minutes for participants to discuss it and record their answers.

4. Have two small groups merge to share their answers. They will prepare a summary, which will then be shared with the other merged groups.

Extending the Activity:

1. Collect statistics/predictions/quotations relevant to either the field in which participants work or the course you are facilitating. Use these as the basis for group and whole-class discussions, just as the entries on Worksheet #12-2 were used.

2. If possible, invite a futurist to share his or her insights with the class.

Workplace Connections:

1. Encourage participants to keep in touch with at least one other member of the class (allow time to exchange e-mail or work phone numbers). Keeping in touch in this case will mean a bi-monthly connection in which the participants discuss interesting statistics or current events that might impact the way they will work in the future.

2. Suggest a benchmarking project to participants. They will make arrangements to learn what others in similar industries or similar positions are doing to deal with emerging realities. The report that is prepared from the benchmarking study should be shared with a wide workplace audience.

Questions for Further Consideration:

1. How has your job changed (whether or not you have been doing it) over the last ten years?

2. Did you foresee those changes? Explain why or why not.

3. Who in your work environment really keeps abreast of advances in your field? Why do you think he or she does this?

4. What do you think is meant by Warren Bennis's assertion that the factory of the future will have only two living beings in it: a dog to prevent people from touching the equipment, and a man to feed the dog?

5. America has moved from an industrial nation to a service economy. What other changes do you think will occur over the next century?

Directions: When we work to organize information, it helps if we can find commonalities among seemingly disparate pieces of information. A fun way to help sharpen your find-the-common-thread wits is called "stratification." You will be given three words (i.e., head, roll, and on) and asked to find another word that has some connection to the first three. The word you are looking for might go in front of or behind each of the other three. For the three words just given, the answer is "egg"—egghead, egg roll, and egg on.

Answer:

_____	1. tired	bone	gone
_____	2. up	sure	known
_____	3. play	under	town
_____	4. out	play	down
_____	5. life	light	stalker
_____	6. outer	upper	bread
_____	7. chase	tiger	clip
_____	8. coat	dream	boat
_____	9. foot	beach	basket
_____	10. clause	quick	artist
_____	11. super	goldfish	soup
_____	12. nip	walk	fish
_____	13. belly	soup	pie
_____	14. coat	split	brain
_____	15. race	side	hog
_____	16. big	steering	barrow
_____	17. dead	put	gun
_____	18. turtle	lace	polo
_____	19. call	book	pay
_____	20. mark	case	check

Try making up some of your own. You'll enjoy flexing your mental muscles this way. What's more, though, you'll be able to share them with friends, associates, and family members.

Directions: Select any one cluster of information and discuss it with your teammates. Then prepare, as a team, either a brief prediction of how the information cited may impact the future or a prediction about a trend that seems to be emerging.

CLUSTER A:

In late 2002, an average of 57,000 jobs a month were lost in the manufacturing sector, but in January of 2003, that number dropped to 16,000 jobs lost. ** More Americans work in the movie industry, according to Nuala Beck, than work in the automotive industry. ** Over 80% of the technological advances in the world have occurred in the last 100 years.

_____

_____

_____

CLUSTER B:

Life expectancy has increased by six years since 1970. ** The planet is 7 million years old, but its population did not reach a billion until 1860. 75 years later, the population had doubled. By 1975, it doubled again, this time in only 50 years. ** "If you have always done it that way, it is probably wrong," wrote Charles Kettering.

_____

_____

_____

CLUSTER C:

"Progress might have been all right once, but it has gone on too long," quipped Ogden Nash. ** 60 billion faxes are produced each year. ** Faster, smaller, cheaper. ** Adapt or die.

_____

_____

_____

CLUSTER D:

750 million computer-generated pages are printed each day. ** "We are drowning in information but starved for knowledge!" wrote John Naisbitt. ** 95% of all information is stored on paper.

_____

_____

_____

Overview:	Creative thought is new thought. With this activity, participants are encouraged to think new thoughts about the work being done in their organizations. Working in teams, they will critically examine current practices and ways to ameliorate them.
Objective:	To engage participants in the process of improving how individuals, teams, and organizations get things done.
Supplies:	• Transparency #13-1 • Overhead projector • Flipcharts (ideally, one per table group)
Time:	15–20 minutes
Advance Preparation:	Download Transparency #13-1. Arrange seating, if possible, so participants can sit in table groups of five or six.
Participants/ Application:	This exercise can accommodate any number of participants. It works best either at the very beginning of the training as an over-arching framework for continuous learning/continuous improvement imperatives, or at the end of the training session, to summarize the need for lifelong learning.

Introduction to Concept:

Educator Rudolph Flesch once commented, "Creative thinking may simply mean the realization that there is no particular virtue in doing things the way they have always been done." There is, by contrast, a distinct virtue in doing things the way they have not always been done. Good examples can be found in the book by Robert Kriegel, *If It Ain't Broke, Break It: Unconventional Wisdom for a Business World.*

In fact, the philosophy behind the popular Total Quality Management (TQM) movement is a philosophy that stresses continuous improvement. Continuous improvement means continuous change. If you do not possess the particular virtue of being able to break away from traditional thinking, you may be putting your job, your team, your department, and possibly even your organization in jeopardy. Quality advocates assure us that if you always do what you've always done, you'll always have what you've already got. And what you've already got might not be enough to remain competitive in this mercurial business climate.

Examples:

The business world abounds with leaders for whom "good enough" simply was not. To cite but a few:

Jack Stack, CEO of Springfield Remanufacturing, author of *The Great Game of Business,* advocates letting every employee know exactly what he or she costs the company and exactly what they are adding to the company's bottom line.

In *Job Shift,* author **Bill Bridges** talks about a "dejobbed future" and asserts that while there will always be work, there will not always be jobs as they have been defined in the past. He uses as an example the country's largest producer of kayaks. This is a firm with only one employee, the owner, who "outsources" or turns over to other firms the various subprocesses that constitute the manufacture of these sleek canoes.

Author **David Armstrong,** by way of his book's title, *Managing by Storying Around,* has coined a new term for managers and leaders everywhere. This "new" tool represents a simple, memorable, fun, and timeless means of informing people about business matters.

Procedure:

1. Form teams of five or six participants and ask each team to list on chart paper ten specific things (policies, procedures, philosophies, processes, paperwork, practices, meetings, etc.) that they (or their team, their department, their company) have been doing the same way for a long time.

2. Encourage brainstorming on any or all of the following [show Transparency #13-1]:

    The opposite of those certain ways

    An addition to those ten ways of doing things

    A subtraction from those ten ways of doing things

    An alteration of those ten ways of doing things

    The elimination of at least one of those ten ways of doing things
    (What would replace traditional meetings, for example?)

    A combination of some of those ten ways of doing things

3. Call on one person in each team to share some of the workable ideas that evolve from their working session.

Extending the Activity:

1. In corporate America, employees undergo 360° evaluations—assessments of their performance are made not only by their supervisors, but also by their co-workers, their customers, their subordinates (if they have any), and often by the employees themselves. A decade ago, such an appraisal reversal would have been unheard of. To encourage break-away-from-tradition thinking and to make participants realize that they have grown comfortable with procedures that truly were unheard of years ago, compile a list of ways things have changed radically.

    Begin with such things as new smoking laws, which do not permit smoking on flights or in most offices. Add to the list the fact that in many workplaces, women were not permitted to wear slacks as recently as the 1970s. Self-directed work teams, benchmarking initiatives, and most of today's organizational policies and procedures are relatively new, to say nothing of the technology we find so indispensable.

    To make the exercise more interactive, use prompts such as, "When was the first time you used a fax machine?" "What year do you remember first having a woman as a supervisor?"

2. Have available copies of books (such as those cited in this activity) that promote the idea of breakaway thinking, an integral element in critical thought. Periodically pass a book to a participant, ask him or her to skim the book to find one workable idea or one valuable quote, and continue with the lesson. Five minutes later, return to the person and ask him or her to share the idea he or she has found.

Workplace Connections:

1. Thomas Alva Edison forced himself to come up with ten new ideas each month and one invention every six months. Ask participants to form informal think tanks when they return to work. The collective goal would be to generate at least ten new ideas each month, the best of which will be shared with supervisors once every six months.

2. Suggest that employees keep a simple journal in which they log the improvements, however minor, that they have made to the work and work processes in which they are engaged. Then, a week or so before their annual performance review, they will extract the most significant of those improvements, type them up, and have them ready to share with their supervisor during the appraisal meeting.

Questions for Further Consideration:

1. What do you think is meant by Tom Peters' claim, "If you have gone a whole week without being disobedient, you are doing your organization and yourself a disservice"?

2. How are those who defy tradition treated in your organization?

3. Historically, how have tradition-defiers been treated?

4. Would you agree with the statement that leaders are change agents? Tell why or why not.

5. What can you do to increase your co-workers' willingness to find a better way of doing the work they do?

6. Think about your own work area. What are some improvements that are needed? Which improvement would have the best payoff?

7. What are the first steps you would need to undertake in order to create the improved reality?

8. What, if anything, may be preventing you from taking these steps?

9. How would you, your co-workers, the department, and the organization itself each benefit from this improvement?

10. How would you interpret this observation by author Roger Dawson: "If Edison had been a CEO of a conglomerate, he probably would have insisted upon the invention of the world's best oil lantern instead of inventing the light bulb."?

Alternatives to Tradition

- The opposite of those certain ways

- An addition to those ten ways

- A subtraction from those ten ways

- An alteration of those ten ways

- The elimination of at least one of those ten ways of doing things (What could replace traditional meetings, for example?)

- A combination of some of those ten ways of doing things

Overview:	Participants will have to move around in this exercise. They will select a pair of shoes, read a self-revealing statement by and about the shoes' owner, and then view a problem from this person's perspective.
Objective:	To develop creative thinking by viewing a problem from an unusual perspective.
Supplies:	• 3" x 5" cards (one for each participant) • Flipchart • Aerosol can of room deodorizer (optional)
Time:	About 15 minutes
Advance Preparation:	None required.
Participants/ Application:	This exercise works with any size group. In terms of sequence, it makes an idea-energizer or session stimulator. It is not recommended as a session starter, however, for it may cause some participants to erroneously assume the entire training sessions will be comprised of "touchy-feely" activities.

Introduction to Concept:

Some of the best ideas evolve from a thinker's ability to put him- or herself in the mind of someone else or to make unusual connections. For example, an architect once described architecture as "frozen music." And when management guru Peter Drucker was asked by a young manager how he could become an outstanding manager, Drucker replied, "Learn to play the violin." By focusing on an altogether new set of circumstances, by viewing work life from an entirely new perspective, we can acquire fresh insights into existing practices.

Examples:

When Jonas Salk was asked how he discovered the vaccine for polio, he replied, "I learned to think the way Mother Nature thinks." When former San Francisco Giants coach Wes Westrum was asked his views on the game of baseball, he thought as a man-of-the-cloth would think: "It's like church. Many attend, but few understand." And when sportswriter Roger Kahn was asked to describe the sport of kings, he declared, "Horse racing is animated roulette."

Procedure:

1. Pose a problem to the class or present an issue that is likely to concern them—as employees, as learners, as leaders, as parents, as citizens, as earth-dwellers, etc. Write this on the whiteboard or flipchart. Or ask them to decide on one organizational issue that concerns most of them.

2. Take off your shoes and ask others to do the same. Make a show of spraying the aerosol scent.

3. Write a sentence that describes yourself (not physically, but rather psychologically or mentally) and place it in your shoes. Ask others to do the same.

4. Ask participants to put on (or at least select) the shoes of some other person, as you look for a pair that fits you.

5. Now have participants view the problem from the perspective of the other person—using not only the sentences in the shoes, but also what the shoe-holder may know or can rightfully assume about that person. He or she, for example, could be:

    –   Someone who is an athlete
    –   Someone of the opposite sex
    –   Someone who is interested in music
    –   Someone who is very concerned with fashion
    –   Someone who loves animals, and so on

6. Participants will jot down their thoughts about the issue from the perspective of the shoe-owner. (The perspective, again, will be determined by the sentence in the shoe, by what the person actually knows about the shoe-holder, or by what the person has assumed about the shoe-owner.)

7. After the shoes are returned to their original owners, small teams will share their new insights acquired by putting themselves "in another person's shoes" and will select a solution they feel could best solve the problem.

8. A spokesperson from each team will report on the ideas.

Extending the Activity:

1. Compile a diverse list of people whose work requires a lot of thinking—a CEO, a police officer, an entrepreneur, a college student, a scientist, a musician, a team leader, an activist, a politician, a warehouse foreman, etc.—and as problems arise for classroom consideration, have participants think as if they were in the shoes of one of these persons.

2. Take a given problem and encourage participants to view it from new perspectives—quite literally. Stimulate creativity with queries such as these:

    "What if we were looking at this problem ten years from now?"
    "What if we were looking at this problem from a bird's eye view?"
    "What if we were looking at this problem from a worm's eye view?"
    "What if we were looking at this problem as Europeans?"
    "What if we were looking at this problem from outer space?"

"What if we were looking at this problem as we marched to the tune
of a different drummer?"

"What if we were looking at this problem while working in the world's
best-equipped science lab?"

Workplace Connections:

1. Strongly advise participants to use a variation of this activity at their next staff or team meeting. The meeting leader distributes a 3" x 5" card to each member present. On the card, meeting attendees write a word that describes what they are outside of work. Ask them to avoid common responses, such as "mother" or "father," but use instead a word(s) that reflects other dimensions of their persona: "avid sportsman," for example, or "reader of mystery novels." The meeting leader will collect the cards and, as discussion is held on particular issues or problems, the leader will pull out a card and ask, "How might an avid sportsman view this issue or solve this problem?" and encourage discussion.

2. Suggest that participants keep a weekly log in which they will record all the problems they have to solve or decisions they have to make at work. At the end of each day, they should place a star in front of those problems/decisions of greater import, ones that do not have to be solved or made "on the spot." Typically, such issues have some temporal leeway.

   For long-term issues, participants should locate three individuals (inside or outside their organizations) who can offer unusual perspectives on the problem or decision. Ideally, these individuals will function in a way that is markedly different from the way in which the participant functions. (Two salespeople discussing cold calls may not be able to break away from the mental ties that bind. But one salesperson discussing cold calls with an undertaker or a hospital administrator is more likely to have fresh insights.)

Questions for Further Consideration:

1. IdeaVerse at AT&T is a place employees can go to in order to have their mental muscles massaged. The walls are purple, the chairs are made of beans, and the ceiling has paintings on it. How would you decorate a room that invites employees to nurture their creative potential?

2. What barriers prevent people from exploring their creative sides?

3. What's the difference between "creativity" and "innovation"?

4. What's the down-side of creativity?

5. Experts assert that if your job is not aligned with your creative style, you may be crippling yourself. How and/or why could this be so?

6. Has downsizing reduced thinking time in your organization? If so, how can it be restored, even in small spurts? If it has not been reduced, how/when/where does thinking and discussion about such issues take place?

7. Although micromanagers or taskmasters would be appalled at the thought, the Microsoft company sets aside Friday afternoons as play time. Such a policy may not be feasible where you work, but a modification of it might. What could you do to make the workplace more enjoyable? (Go beyond the obvious answers.)

8. List ten individuals in your organization whom you know and would describe as "powerful" for one reason or another. Would you describe their thinking style as "creative" or "cautious"? How has this style propelled or impaired the career progress of each?

Overview:	In this exercise, participants will review a set of turnaround phrases, create one of their own, and then vote to select their favorite from the posted creations.
Objective:	To present participants with problematic situations and give them an opportunity to view them critically and create possible solutions.
Supplies:	• Colored adhesive circles, one for each participant • Handout #15-1 • Four apple turnovers (optional) (**Note:** If the turnovers are used, it is best to present the activity just before the mid-morning break.)
Time:	15 minutes
Advance Preparation:	Purchase a box of adhesive circles (and apple turnovers, if you wish). Make copies of the handout, to be distributed to each participant. Arrange seating in triads, if possible.
Participants/ Application:	If used as a warm-up, this exercise substantiates the reason participants are in the training: to develop skills that will enable them to solve problems they are bound to encounter at work. If used as an energizer, the favored turnaround could be woven into the context of the lessons that remain. If used as a session-closer, the turnarounds could be used to answer the questions, "What next?" and "Where do we go from here?" There is no limit to the number of triads that could work in this exercise. (If one or two participants are left over, they each can join a three-person team.)

Introduction to Concept:

Verbal turnarounds are sentences that turn around the thought expressed in the first half in order to offer optimism in the second half. Such statements, admittedly difficult to create, often serve as inspirational forces. They can also suggest possible solutions to a problem or new paths to be followed.

We are often so intent on solving our problems that we fail to establish the context within which the solution can most effectively be found. By articulating the attitude necessary for the poking and prodding of the problem, we can establish the framework that aids us in generating solutions and selecting the most promising among them.

Procedure:

1. Divide the class into triads.

2. Have participants, working in triads, make a list of ten sentences reflecting issues they are concerned about and/or interested in, or problems they have to solve, or major decisions they have to make regarding work.

3. Distribute Handout #15-1, give participants about five minutes to read the entries, and then ask if everyone understands what a turnaround phrase is. Explain, if necessary.

4. Collect each group's ten sentences and give them to a different group.

5. Now ask the triads to turn around at least one statement made by the first group. They will do so by making the first half of the sentence a declaration and the second half (or second sentence) an expansion/extension of the declaration. (If a team is stuck, review the handout examples with them once again. If necessary, ask them to create a turnaround of their own, without having to rely on the prompt from another group.)

6. Post the contributions along a wall.

7. Give each person one adhesive circle and ask him or her to apply it to the turnaround sentence he or she likes best.

8. Reward the winning triad with apple turnovers or some other token reward.

Extending the Activity:

1. President Jimmy Carter once observed, "America did not invent civil rights. Civil rights invented America." Collect powerful statements such as this and use them as discussion starters for various classroom topics. President Carter's turnaround, as an example, would work quite well in a class dealing with sexual harassment or cultural diversity issues.

2. H. L. Mencken once remarked, "For every complex problem, there is one solution that is simple, neat... and wrong." Lead a discussion with the class regarding serious consequences that have resulted from hasty decisions. Then explore how turnaround statements —which set up the mental and physical framework necessary for successful solutions— can prevent us from leaping at solutions that are "simple, neat... and wrong."

Workplace Connections:

1. Once participants have diagnosed the problem and fashioned a context for its solution, the next step is to create an action plan for the turnaround sentence. For example, assume that your company's purchasing department has instituted a number of changes regarding the purchasing policy. The turnaround may have been, "If vendors refuse to change, we may have to change vendors." The workplace follow-up, then, would be outlining the steps necessary to do that.

2. Ask for a volunteer, ideally one with some artistic talent, to take the winning entry, fashion it into mini-banners or certificates that can be hung in the workplace, and then distribute them to the participants who were part of this training program.

Questions for Further Consideration:

1. What phrases from some of our national leaders do you remember?

2. What makes such phrases memorable?

3. What does this turnaround by Seneca mean to you: "It is not because things are difficult that we do not dare; it is because we do not dare that things are difficult"?

4. Parents are often the source of inspirational phrases, even though they are not turn-arounds. For example, "health is wealth" is a reminder all of us have to keep in mind. What other succinct wisdom were you exposed to in your formative years?

5. Does your organization have a motto, such as the one Thomas Watson, Jr., gave to IBM ("Think!") or the one Sam Walton wanted his employees to abide by ("Eliminate the dumb!")? If so, what is it and how accepted is it? If there is none, what motto would you create for your firm?

6. What uses can you think of for the turnaround statements created in this training session?

Directions: Study the following turnaround phrases. Note that they posit a potential problem in the first half of the sentence, and a potential solution in the second half.

Jesse Jackson: "I was born in the slums but the slums were not born in me."

Winston Churchill: "The pessimist sees difficulty in every opportunity; the optimist sees opportunity in every difficulty."

Anonymous: "When the going gets tough, the tough get going."

LeRoy Satchel Paige: "Age is a question of mind over matter. If you don't mind, it doesn't matter."

Vitamin ad: "It may not add years to your life but it can add life to your years."

Joseph Joubert: "It is better to debate a question without settling it than to settle a question without debating it."

Anonymous: "How a problem defeats you is less important than how you defeat the problem."

Sam Keen: "We have to move from the illusion of certainty to the certainty of illusion."

Anonymous: "It's nice to be important but it's more important to be nice."

Robert Bolton: "A belief is not merely an idea the mind possesses; it is an idea that possesses the mind."

A. N. Whitehead: "The art of progress is to preserve order amid change and to preserve change amid order."

Winston Churchill: "This is not the end. It is not even the beginning of the end. But it is, perhaps, the end of the beginning."

Overview: Participants will take a test that reveals which hemisphere of the brain dominates their thinking and will then work in groups to generate creative responses to a hypothetical prompt.

Objective: To provide participants with information regarding their personal thinking styles.

Supplies: Copies of Worksheet #16-1, one per participant
(**Note:** At first, only half of the participants will receive the worksheet.)

Time: 15–20 minutes

Advance Preparation: Make copies of the worksheet. Arrange the seating so pairs can work together. Because the second half of the exercise requires participants to be divided into three groups, it is best to have tables for them, if possible. Write these prompts on the flipchart but keep them covered until the second half of the activity:

- If women ruled the world…
- If elephants could fly…
- If the average life span were 150 years…
- If 95% of secretaries were men instead of women…
- If personal computers cost $10.00…
- If we wanted to live underwater…

Participants/ Application: There is no limit to the number of participants who can work on this activity, but there should be at least 12 participants, given the nature of the tasks in which they will be engaged. The exercise can be used as a warm-up activity at the very beginning of the training program when fear or discomfort may be overshadowing the natural enthusiasm for learning. It can also be used to boost attention any time during the training day. Relate the exercise to whatever subject you are facilitating by pointing out the need for continuous improvement of our cognitive abilities.

Introduction to Concept:

By now, most of you have heard the phrases "left brain" and "right brain" in reference to the way we think. Sometimes, jokes are made about our thinking orientation (left-brain dominance equals analytical thinking; right-brain dominance equals creative thinking). And yet numerous Fortune 500 companies are investing in training that teaches employees how to combine detail and logic (left-lobe functions) with vision and inventiveness (right-lobe functions).

When right-brainers are forced to work in left-brained situations (and vice versa), considerable stress ensues. If for no other reason than your own good health, you should know how your brain works. And if you are unable or unwilling to achieve lateralization (equal use of both lobes), you should make sure the orientation of your thinking parallels the orientation of your workplace.

Procedure:

1. Divide the class into pairs. (If one person is left over, he or she can work as your partner, in which case you would give him or her the test on the worksheet). If possible, have the partners facing each other.

2. Distribute Worksheet #16-1 TO ONLY ONE PARTNER IN EACH PAIR. Explain that the person being tested will figure out the answers in his or her head rather than with paper and pencil. Allow a few moments for the test-giver to read the two paragraphs at the top of the worksheet and then to conduct the test with his or her partner.

3. When the test is complete, give a copy of it to the "testee," so he or she can use it with others in the future. Tell the testees to form three groups: one for those who turned out to be lateralized, one for those who had six or more check marks in the "left" column (meaning they favor their creative side), and a third group for those who had six or more checks in the "right" column (meaning they are more "right-brain" dependent).

4. As the groups are assembling, call the test-givers together and give them this simple instruction: "I want you to sit now in a very relaxed position, with your hands folded in your lap." [Pause.] Now look down at your hands. If the left thumb is on top, please join the group that had a majority of check marks in the 'left' column. If your right thumb is on top, please join the group that had a majority of check marks in the 'right' column. And if you had your thumbs side by side, you will join the 'lateralized' group."

5. Once the groups are assembled, present the flipchart questions. Explain that they will have exactly ten minutes to select one entry and to write as long a list as possible of consequences. In other words, what would logically happen if the "if" possibility were a reality?

6. Compare the length of the lists from the three groups. They should be about equal, in that this exercise calls for both creative and analytical thinking. (The lateralized group will have these skills in equal measure, so their lists should be as long as the others are.) If one group did exceptionally well, ask participants what factors (for example, the size of the group) might account for their results.

Extending the Activity:

1. Collect articles on the topics of creativity, left-brain/right-brain research, and learning organizations. Distribute one to every two participants. Give them five minutes to scan the articles to find one workable idea or one interesting concept. At the end of five minutes, call on one person in each pair to share their selections.

2. In round-robin fashion, call on each person to tell either what has helped him or her to foster creative thinking or what barriers (self-imposed or otherwise) prevent him or her from thinking creatively. As participants share their thoughts, record the gist of them on the flipchart. Make two columns. In the first, list the creativity-drivers and in the second, the creativity-barriers. Then lead a discussion regarding ways to reduce the number in the second column.

Workplace Connections:

1. Recommend that employees periodically rent, purchase, or preview videos on creativity, ideally during the lunch hour, and hold discussions afterwards to determine how to use what was learned in their everyday work lives.

2. Ask participants to sign up for a sequel to the course you have just facilitated. The sequel will be a half-day or one-day program they themselves designed. Each participant will teach a ten-minute chunk about ways creativity can be increased. You will be responsible for designing the curriculum for the remaining time.

Questions for Further Consideration:

1. What circumstances in the formative years of a human being lead to later creative behavior?

2. What circumstances lead to diminished creative behavior?

3. How do you feel about author Max DePree's assertion that "anything truly creative results in change, and if there is one thing a well-run major corporation finds difficult to handle, it is change"?

4. What evidence do you see that your organization (or others that you know of) is working to develop innovative thought among employees?

5. What is the procedure in your workplace by which processes are improved?

Directions: Sit in front of your partner. Do not let him or her see this paper. Read the directions to yourself before giving your partner the test. Do NOT read these directions aloud. Explain that you are going to ask ten questions. You are actually not at all concerned about the answers given because… YOU ARE GOING TO WATCH THE PERSON'S EYES TO SEE IN WHICH DIRECTION HE OR SHE FIRST GLANCES WHEN WORKING OUT THE ANSWER.

Place a check in the appropriate column below. If the person glances to his or her left, check the left column. Similarly, check the right column if the person glances immediately to his or her right, or if the person glances up and then to the right. If your partner does not look in either direction, do not check either box. Now you're ready to read the questions to your partner.

	LEFT	RIGHT
1. How many letters are there in the words "critical thinking?"	❏	❏
2. How many pointed corners are there in a cube?	❏	❏
3. What was the name of your favorite grade school teacher?	❏	❏
4. Multiply 19 times 8 in your head.	❏	❏
5. Name the letters of the alphabet that are curved when written as capital letters.	❏	❏
6. Give three meanings for the word "set."	❏	❏
7. What did you have for dinner last night?	❏	❏
8. As you go from the front of this building to your work site, how many corridors do you pass through?	❏	❏
9. Tell me which numbers from 1 to 100 are pronounced with an "ee" sound.	❏	❏
10. As you look at a quarter, in which direction is George Washington facing?	❏	❏

Analysis: If your partner had a score of 5/5 or he or she was looking straight ahead as he or she answered five or more questions, then the person is probably "lateralized." This means he or she has learned to use both hemispheres of the brain equally well.

If your partner had six or more in the "left" column, he or she probably has a right-brain bias. (The direction in which they glance is opposite to the hemisphere that is active at the time.) This means he or she is more intuitive, more artistic, more creative, more emotional, more visual, more spatially adroit, more entrepreneurial, and more holistic in his or her thinking than the average person is. Those who rely upon the right-side of their brains are frequently poets, dreamers, innovators.

If your partner had a score of six or more in the right column, he or she is more oriented to left-brain thinking than the average person. Such individuals are logical, reasonable, quantitative in their thinking, analytical, detailed, and well-organized. They make excellent lawyers, accountants, supervisors, and engineers.

Overview:	Two tests comprise this activity. In the first, based on the work of Harvard's David McClelland, participants select an interpretation based on their motivational needs, which ideally are aligned with the work they are doing. In the second, participants learn more about their critical-thinking orientation. Ideally, again, the kind of work they do for a living is matched with their thinking preferences.
Objective:	To enable participants to learn more about their work-related preferences.
Supplies:	• Copies of Worksheet #17-1, one per participant • Copies of Handout #17-1, one per participant
Time:	25–30 minutes
Advance Preparation:	Make copies of the worksheets and the handouts.
Participants/ Application:	This exercise is adaptable to any size group. It works well as an energizer and especially well as an introductory exercise, reinforcing the need for participants to learn as much as they can about their own orientations (emotional and intellectual) in order to ensure the best possible job fit.

Introduction to Concept:

Part I: A recent study (reported in the September 1996 issue of Solutions, page 11) revealed the primary reason why corporate managers are terminated. As you might guess, it is not because they lack the requisite skills. (Without them, they probably would not have been promoted to the position in the first place.) The top reason, according to Manchester Partners International, sponsor of the survey, is that they are mismatched with their positions. When people are stuck in their roles as technicians, the study points out, they are unable to think in a more visionary, strategic manner. According to Dr. Elliott Ross, a consulting psychologist for the division that conducted the study, organizations must "do a better job of identifying the competencies that people require to be more successful now, and in the future."

The short test you are going to take now is only a first step in the process of identifying your competencies and then ensuring that they are matched to the requirements of the job you perform. [Pause here and distribute Worksheet #17-1. After participants have made their selections, continue with Part II of the mini-lecture.]

Part II: For more than forty years, Professor David McClelland of Harvard has conducted research on the kind of motivation that drives us to perform our very best work. Some people, he has learned, are driven by a need for power. Others are driven by a need to work with other people, a need he refers to as "affiliation." Finally, some people work best in a situation that allows them to achieve because of their individual efforts, rather than the collective efforts of others. You can learn more about the three motivational drives from this handout. [Distribute Handout #17-1.]

Procedure:

1. Distribute Worksheet #17-1 and ask participants to select the scenario they feel best describes the illustration. Once they have made their selections, continue with Part II of the Introduction.

2. Distribute Handout #17-1 and lead a discussion based on whether or not people agree with these initial assessments of their motivations. Ask those who found the assessment accurate whether the work they currently do matches the preference indicated by their choices on Worksheet #17-1. If not, ask if they have ever thought about doing a different kind of work—perhaps when they retire.

3. Emphasize that the more we know about our preferences (occupational, cognitive, etc.), the more easily we can fit our interests to our livelihood. Then explain that you have one more test to give them. Assure participants that there are no right or wrong answers. They will surely be learning more about their thinking styles.

Extending the Activity:

1. Ask someone from the personnel department to discuss the use of psychological testing as part of the interview process.

2. If you or another facilitator is familiar with the administration of the Myers-Briggs personality tests, allow time for participants to take the tests and then to study the results.

Workplace Connections:

1. Suggest that participants spend some time discovering more about their own thinking style or preferred manner of executing work-related tasks. Then suggest they spend time doing a similar assessment for their immediate supervisor. If there is considerable variance, advise them to forge a partnership with their supervisor that reduces misunderstanding or supplements the "weaknesses" of each partner.

2. Because the research shows high numbers of people whose careers do not parallel their passions, suggest that participants meet with career counselors or take other tests that indicate their job preferences. If there are incongruities between what they do and what they like to do, have participants discuss with their supervisors possible transfers to other positions within the organization.

Questions for Further Discussion:

1. Dr. Joyce Brothers created the term "the Lockheed Syndrome" to describe the thinking style of engineers; she suggests it is distinct and different from that of non-engineers. Would you agree with her opinion? Tell why or why not.

2. What path led you to the job you hold today?

3. What advice would you give to young people trying to find their occupational niche in the world?

4. Describe your parents' career decisions as compared to your own.

5. How will impending changes impact how you work and what you work on?

Directions: After looking at each illustration, select the scenario that you feel most closely approximates what you think might be happening in the picture.

1)

   a) George is an accomplished performer and has recently been hired for an off-Broadway play. He is only inches away now from his ultimate goal.

   b) George has organized a musical review to celebrate his company's achievement of ISO certification (an international quality standard). His team is not only performing, it is also serving refreshments to the assembled guests.

   c) George is concerned about the senior citizens at a nursing home where his aunt is a resident who never seems to have visitors. He is putting on a song-and-dance routine for them, complete with jokes he has made up.

2)

   a) Cynthia's recent promotion meant a transcontinental move, but one she didn't mind making. She's packed all her valuables, fastened the seat belt around the cocker spaniel beside her, and is shoving off to Buffalo.

   b) As manager of a hard-working staff, Cynthia has organized a wilderness retreat in order for the staff to do some strategic planning without typical office interruptions. She's thought of everything they'll need (including laptops, fax machine, printer, and even a small copier) to make the session a success.

   c) Cynthia is on her way to a family reunion in Colorado. It's been twelve long months since she's seen her relatives, and she couldn't be more excited.

3)

   a) Tony is making a sales pitch to his most important client.

   b) Tony is giving a pep talk to his staff, hoping to sell the concept of empowerment to them.

   c) At the retirement party he has organized for a fellow clerk, Tony is making a few remarks about how valuable she has been to the department.

Directions: Which answer—a, b, or c—did you select more than once?

If you selected (a) more than once, you have a strong need for Achievement.

You place a very high value on such things as the ability to work independently. You prefer a job that allows you the freedom to make your own decisions and control your own destiny. You would do well as an entrepreneur, making the business grow as you see fit. You would also do well in a position that permits autonomy (such as a professor) rather than in a position that is bound by many rules and regulations (such as a manager in a corporation).

If you selected (b) more than once, you have a strong need for Power.

Thank goodness there are people like you around. Otherwise, America would never have won a war and corporations would not be able to report profits to their shareholders. Those with a need for power make excellent managers. They like to get things done through the efforts of those whom they manage or lead. You enjoy being in a position of authority. You value getting done what you are paid to do more than you enjoy developing close personal relationships.

If you selected (c) more than once, you have a strong need for Affiliation.

Individuals who value positive relationships in the workplace are driven by a strong need for affiliation. The thing they typically like best about their jobs is the people with whom they work. They feel a need to resolve office conflicts so positive morale can be restored to the workplace. Typically, persons with a high need for affiliation do not enjoy work that is supervisory in nature.

If you selected (a) once, (b) once, and (c) once, there is no clear indication of your motivation preference and further tests are warranted.

Overview:	Critical thought is promoted through this exercise, which asks participants to assess possibilities and then determine if presented scenarios are real or fabricated.
Objective:	To increase participants' awareness of the need to verify information—no matter how creatively intuitive they may be.
Supplies:	• Copies of Worksheet #18-1, one for each participant • Paper and pencil for participants
Time:	About 25 minutes
Advance Preparation:	Make copies of the worksheet. Arrange seating, if possible, so groups of four or five can work together.
Participants/ Application:	Because critical thinking is an integral part of the learning process no matter what training program you may be facilitating, this exercise works well as a tone-setter at the beginning of the program. It can also be used as a session-stimulator, for lively exchanges inevitably ensue from the discussions of the examples and also from the creation of comparable scenarios.

Introduction to Concept:

Professor Weston Agor at the University of Texas asserts that because we live in a fast-changing, megatrend world, creative intuition is probably more important to survival today than it ever was in the past. What is "creative intuition"? What does he mean by "logical" intuition and how can you tell if you have it?

Let's begin with a definition of intuition itself: "The ability to perceive or know something without conscious reasoning." We can either be "logically" intuitive or "creatively" intuitive. Logical intuition assists us in analyzing what we do know, from direct or indirect experience, and using that knowledge to weigh the validity of our intuitive feelings. Creative intuition often begins in whimsy or fantasy and ends with an idea that we feel, intuitively, will work in a given situation.

Worksheet #18-1 presents you with a number of scenarios, some of which are true and others that are completely fabricated. Working with others in your group, you will discuss, logically, the likelihood that the scenario is true and indicate your choice ("true" or "false") beneath each scenario. Later, I will share the results that will tell if your team is, as a whole, logically intuitive or not. [Distribute the worksheet now.]

Procedure:

1. Divide the class into an even number of small groups and distribute the worksheet. After participants have finished it, share the answers with them: All the scenarios are true except #3. Point out that if the groups were consistently correct, they probably have a collective logical intuition. If consistently wrong, they may be too closed in their thinking.

2. Ask each team now to look around the room and to select one other group with whom they will partner. [Each group should have a different partner group.]

3. Tell the teams to look at their partners and think about what they know or have perceived about the members of the partner group so far. The teams will then begin to work on this task, which you will share with them as follows:

> Based on what you know or have perceived about the thinking styles of the individuals in your partnership team, would they be more likely to think an unusual story is true or false? Use your intuition and your hunches, as there really is no way of telling how a given group will respond to a given scenario. We can only predict. As a team, you will use your intuition to predict the way the other team is most likely to vote. Use your creativity, too: actually imagine them reading your unusual story. How might they react?

> After discussing and agreeing upon the more likely vote ("true" or "false") in response to a story, your team will do the opposite of the vote. In other words, if you intuitively feel the partner team would vote "true," then you as a team will fabricate, in writing, a very unusual story, perhaps like the ones you read about or like the urban legends you may have heard about. But if you feel your partners would vote "false," then you are to record a true story or experience that one of you has had.

4. When the stories are complete, have the teams exchange them and vote on the stories they receive. Poll the teams to learn whose intuition (about how the other team would vote) was correct.

Extending the Activity:

1. Ask if anyone feels he or she is especially intuitive. [**Note:** If no one admits to it, give this short quiz anyway.] Explain that the "intuitor" would have no way of knowing the answers— you simply want to give him or her a chance to use hunches in response to certain questions. Get the volunteer or appointed intuitor to stand. Give the test aloud, in front of the entire group, and have the intuitor say the answer out loud. Then go back and reveal the correct answers to the entire group. Determine how intuitive the intuitor actually was.

   1) For every one person on earth, how many insects are there? **(7 million)**

   2) What is the height of Mount Kilimanjaro? **(19,340 feet)**

   3) Students of what subject yawn the most? **(calculus students)**

   4) How many students graduate from American high schools each year unable to read the words on their diploma? **(700,000)**

   5) What is the annual cost of medical bills resulting from smoking? **($52 billion)**

   (You could collect other such questions, particularly those related to the subject matter being presented, and use an even longer test with the entire group.)

2. To further test participants' powers of intuition, choose ten unusual words from the dictionary and create a test with two false definitions and one real one.

Workplace Connections:

1. Suggest that participants keep a log for a three-week period to determine if they should place more or less reliance on their gut feelings.

2. Encourage participants to be especially attuned at future staff or team meetings to those individuals (including themselves) who say something akin to "I just have this feeling that it will work." Participants will then keep track of the outcomes of collective decisions that are made—some that go against the intuition of the person who had this feeling and some that concur with the person's feeling. Over an extended period, participants will have sufficient data to give the team or co-workers a summary of the validity of these intuitive reactions to proposed courses of action.

Questions for Further Consideration:

1. Can you recall times when you were glad you relied on your intuition?

2. Can you recall times when you wish you had or hadn't?

3. Do you believe there is such a thing as "woman's intuition?"

4. What role do you think intuition plays in the hiring process? In the process by which you were hired?

5. What process do you use to make decisions?

Directions: Your collective task is to analyze each of these scenarios to the fullest extent possible and assess the likelihood that they are "true" or "false." Write your decisions on the blank lines.

#1. Ben Blumberg, a power systems engineer from Sunnyvale, California, has solved the energy crisis with a stationary bike attached to a small electric generator. If every person in the country pedaled in his or her spare time, our nation would soon be self-sufficient in energy, saving 100 million barrels of oil each year—equivalent to the output of 40 nuclear power plants.

      True or False: _____

#2. The first airline stewardess was Ellen Church, whose maiden flight on United Airlines was on May 15, 1930. She served fruit cocktail, undigestible fried chicken, rolls, and a beverage. She trained seven other unmarried nurses to serve as stewardesses. However, the pilots' wives organized a campaign to have the stewardesses replaced by men.

      True or False: _____

#3. The movie *Jaws* was based on a true experience. Author Peter Benchley was once attacked by a shark while vacationing on Martha's Vineyard. He lost two fingers from his left hand, but that did not prevent him from writing a fictional account of the frightening event. Benchley's book sold 24 million copies.

      True or False: _____

#4. The phrase "flying saucer" was first coined in 1947 by American pilot Kenneth Arnold to describe strange flying machines he had seen over the mountains along the West Coast. His exact words were, "They flew like a saucer would if you skipped it across the water."

      True or False: _____

#5. Flight sergeant Nicholas Alkemade was 21 years old when he made his thirteenth bombing mission over Germany in World War II. He was attacked by a lone Junkers 88. He bailed out 18,000 feet above Berlin without the parachute that had gone up in flames just before he jumped, and survived.

      True or False: _____

#6. The prototype for the game of Monopoly was created by a clergyman's daughter, who called this first American board game "Mansion of Happiness." It remained a popular reminder that good deeds lead to eternal happiness until 16-year-old George Parker converted the game in 1883 from a religious theme to a banking theme.

      True or False: _____

#7. The rickshaw, so prevalent in Japan, was invented in the 1860s by an American Baptist minister named Jonathan Scobie. He devised the two-wheel carriage in order to get his physically handicapped wife out of the house without having to carry her on his back.

      True or False: _____

Overview:	After viewing examples of divergent thinking, participants will work on riddles that help increase "outside-the-box" thinking.
Objective:	To provide participants with a structure for thinking in a non-linear fashion.
Supplies:	• Transparency #19-1 • Overhead projector • Copies of Worksheet #19-1, one per participant
Time:	20 minutes
Advance Preparation:	Download Transparency #19-1. Make copies of the worksheet. Arrange seating, if possible, so table groups of five or six can work together.
Participants/ Application:	This exercise accommodates any number of participants. It can be used at any time during the instructional day, for it begins with humor and then proceeds to the challenges that demand divergent thinking. If used as an introductory exercise, you can stress how both divergent and convergent thinking are required for the kinds of problems participants will face in relation to the training they are now receiving.

Introduction to Concept:

Unimaginative thinkers put a lock on their thinking by taking everything literally. They trap themselves inside the confines of typical, traditional thinking and hesitate to go beyond the known or the obvious. By contrast, those who are mental escape artists unlock the "mindcuffs" that shackle our imaginations the way handcuffs shackle our wrists.

To learn more about divergent thinking, you need only study the responses of children. Asked, for example, how one could get to heaven, most adults would answer in the same way: "By doing good deeds." Not so, children. Their responses, clearly, are not confined to the box labeled "Convergent Thinking." [Show Transparency #19-1.]

Procedure:

1. After showing the transparency, explain that one way to promote creative thinking is to answer and analyze riddles.

2. Divide the class into groups of five or six and distribute the worksheet.

3. After ten minutes or so, ask a volunteer to share his or her group's answers. (Supply the actual answer, if their answers differ. Note that participants' answers may be even better than the actual answers.) The riddle answers are:

    1) A lot of customers

    2) March 4th

    3) It is matchless

    4) I would take the words right out of his mouth

    5) About 25 seconds

    6) Honesty

    7) A hot, cross bunny

    8) Wrinkles

    9) With hare spray

    10) Tie a knot in his tail

    11) Someone who laughs his head off

    12) By playing the flute while surrounded by six cobras, one of which is deaf

4. Take the team through the process of reaching creative responses, using the riddles as a source of explanation. The first step is to discard the obvious, if it even comes into your mind. So, in #1, "If a farmer sold 500 bushels of corn for a dollar a bushel, what would he or she get?" The obvious answer is $500. The divergent answer, the more creative one, does not get to the "correct" answer, which is based on a mathematical calculation. Instead, the divergent answer is based upon the reality of the situation: If you could buy a bushel of corn for a mere dollar, you would probably tell all your friends to visit that farmer!

    In other cases, the answer depends on a double entendre or double meaning. For example, March 4 (Question #2) is a date, but it is also a command to proceed ("March forth"). Double entendres are also plays on words. Such is the case with #3, which asks what makes an empty match box superior to all others. It is "matchless," of course.

    Other divergent answers depend on a familiarity with common phrases. We find this in the fourth question about the dog eating a book: "I would take the words right out of his mouth." Others, like the one about the elephant, depend on your ability to imagine and deal with absurdity.

    Understanding what constitutes creative thought helps us to create it in future circumstances.

Extending the Activity:

1. To encourage further divergent thinking, have participants prepare a long list of popular titles or phrases, such as the hit song, "Girls Just Wanna Have Fun" or Shakespeare's *The Merchant of Venice.* Then ask participants to put creative twists on phrases that business people could use in their advertisements. For example, the first title could be used by a bank seeking more women customers: "Girls Just Wanna Have Funds." A sports equipment enterprise might call the business "The Merchant of Tennis."

2. Divide the class into pairs. Hand each an ordinary object—pencil, staple, paper clip, pipe cleaner, facial tissue, etc. Allocate five minutes and have the teams think of as many uses as possible for the object they have received.

Workplace Connections:

1. Encourage participants to encourage their managers to build in at least five minutes a week for collective brainstorming about work-related problems.

2. Promote the use of "what-could-we-use-this-for" thinking on surpluses that abound in the workplace. For example, "Other than potpourri and sachet bags, how would we re-use the flowers that cover secretaries' desks during Secretaries' Week?"

Questions for Further Consideration:

1. The refusal to "adapt or die" is widely regarded as a prescription for organizational suicide. If you headed your organization, what would you do to discourage employees from clinging to the old when they should be embracing the new?

2. How do idea-pioneers fight for the survival of their ideas?

3. If you were to select a benchmarking partner, one whom you feel could teach you about innovative practices, what company or organization would you choose?

4. Idea-encouragers tell us to seek challenges if we want to be simultaneously critical and creative in our thinking. What in your immediate environment can be improved?

How do you get to heaven?

♣ You go to hell and turn right.

♣ On a trampoline.

♣ By getting the bad spanked out of you.

♣ You fly. It takes three days to get there . . . nonstop.

♣ First you turn into a spirit. From there, it's easy.

♣ You give God a hug. But he's invisible so you fall right through him and land in heaven.

♣ Somebody drives you there in a big black limousine.

♣ Be good and be buried.

Directions: As a group, try to figure out non-obvious answers to these riddles.

1. If a farmer sold 500 bushels of corn for a dollar a bushel, what would he or she get?

     Answer: _____

2. What day of the year is a command to move forward?

     Answer: _____

3. Why is an empty match box superior to all others?

     Answer: _____

4. What would you do if you found a dog eating your book?

     Answer: _____

5. What's the difference between kissing your sister and kissing your sweetheart?

     Answer: _____

6. What is the biggest handicap in gold?

     Answer: _____

7. What do you get when you pour hot water down a rabbit hole?

     Answer: _____

8. What headlines do people like least?

     Answer: _____

9. What is the best way to keep a rabbit in its place?

     Answer: _____

10. How do you keep an elephant from going through the eye of a needle?

     Answer: _____

11. What goes "ha-ha-ha-plop"?

     Answer: _____

12. How do you play Russian roulette in India?

     Answer: _____

Overview: Ten items are presented in this "test," which asks participants to select their preferences from among a series of graphic designs.

Objective: To help participants identify their own artistic inclinations.

Supplies:
- Copies of Worksheet #20-1, one for each participant
- Copies of Handout #20-1, one for each participant
- Transparency #20-1
- Overhead projector
- Flipchart

Time: 15 minutes

Advance Preparation: Make copies of the handout and the worksheet.
Download Transparency #20-1.

Participants/ Application: In a training program *not* related to critical thinking or problem-solving, use this exercise as a warm-up. No matter what results participants wind up with, you can correlate them in this way: "If you found you have a distinct artistic flair, I hope you will use your creativity to contribute your special perspective as we explore various issues related to (*training topic*). Please share your novel insights with us throughout the day—ask questions, offer opinions, even contradict me if you feel what I've said deserves to be challenged. If the results do not show an artistic inclination, just think of the opportunities before you to make that ability as strong as your other abilities are.

You will have many chances today to explore your creative skills. Vow right now to get started. You may even wish to intensify the creative aspects of this training by working as often as you can with someone who did score high—you can see a lot, as Yogi Berra says, "just by observing." If the training is related to critical thinking, you can use the activity any time during the program as a creativity booster. This exercise can be adapted to fit any size group.

Introduction to Concept:

Thinking is an art and creative thinkers must surely be considered artists. How artistic is your thought process? In just a few moments, you will receive a ten-item "test" that will ask for your preference after you view three similar images in each test item. There are no right or wrong answers as such. Instead, you will simply indicate your preference. First, though, we'll do another preference test.

Procedure:

1. Show Transparency #20-1. Allow a few moments for participants to make selections and then offer this amateur-psychologist interpretation:

   - The Ferrari indicates that you prize the speed aspect of critical thinking; the traveling circus equals the creative side; and the little engine reveals the logical end of critical thinking.

   - The bullet train suggests you favor the "quick" part of *The Critical Thinking Tool Kit;* the Orient Express implies a tendency toward creativity; and the rocket trip hints at your analytical nature.

   - The final selection is a bit different. It reveals participants' "lust for life"—or the physical side, with special emphasis on the first noun in the phrase. (Leave further speculation up to the participants themselves.)

   Point out that while this test was a just-for-fun warm-up, the next test will be more serious.

2. Distribute Worksheet #20-1. When everyone has completed it, pass out Handout #20-1 and ask participants to share and discuss their answers with one another.

3. Select a recorder to list key points on the flipchart as you lead a discussion of ways we can increase our artistic abilities: taking courses, reading books, speaking to artists, watching select television programs. If there is any question at all about the value of having business people develop artistic skills, mention that esteemed management authority Peter Drucker advises those who would be outstanding managers to study the violin.

Extending the Activity:

1. On the flipchart, draw these sketches and ask participants to figure out what they are. Solutions will depend on one's creative, fanciful ability to look at things askance.

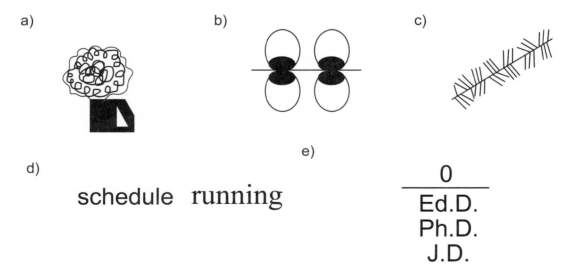

a)

b)

c)

e)

d)

schedule running

$$\frac{0}{\text{Ed.D.}}$$
Ph.D.
J.D.

The answers are: a) an elm tree, b) two olives looking in a mirror, c) a centipede out of step with itself, d) "running behind schedule," and e) "three degrees below zero." Participants can add to the collection, of course. Invite them up to the flipchart or whiteboard to draw their own favorites.

2.   Select a problem or issue that has arisen during the course of the training program and subject it to this analysis with the class as a whole:

   •   What circumstances may have contributed to this situation we are facing?

   •   Which of these problems would you say is most critical?

   •   What are others doing about the same problem?

   •   What are some possible causes of this priority problem?

   •   Which, of all these causes, is probably the most serious? The most likely?

   •   What can we do about the probable cause of the problem?

Workplace Connections:

1.   Encourage participants to select one of the recommendations listed on the flipchart and to pledge to follow through with it upon their return to work. In fact, you could bring closure to the training session by having each participant stand, one at a time, and tell what he or she will follow through with.

2.   Explain to participants that perspectives other than our own help us see things we do not typically see. Suggest that the next time they disagree with or are upset by a decision made by their managers they try to "see," from the manager's eyes, the events leading to the decision.

Questions for Further Consideration:

1.   Why do we have such trouble seeing things from angles that are different from our usual ways of seeing things?

2.   What do you do to dispense with the foolish consistency Emerson described as "the hobgoblin of little minds"?

3.   What are some viewpoints you've heard children express that reveal a refreshingly different slant on life and living?

4.   Do you know or have you heard of someone who "got lucky"? If so, would you ascribe their luck to what Robert Crawford describes as a "sensing of an opportunity—an opportunity that is there for all of us to see"?

How would you describe your thinking style?

- ❏ Ferrari
- ❏ Traveling circus
- ❏ The little engine that could

How would you describe your attitude toward life?

- ❏ A ride on the bullet train
- ❏ A ride on the Orient Express
- ❏ A rocket ride to outer space

Toward which image of water do you gravitate:

- ❏ Icebergs
- ❏ Steam
- ❏ Niagara Falls

Directions: You need only encircle your preference for *one* of the three illustrations in each of the following five items. Don't spend too much time analyzing them, as there are no right or wrong answers. Simply select the one that you seem drawn to, for whatever reason.

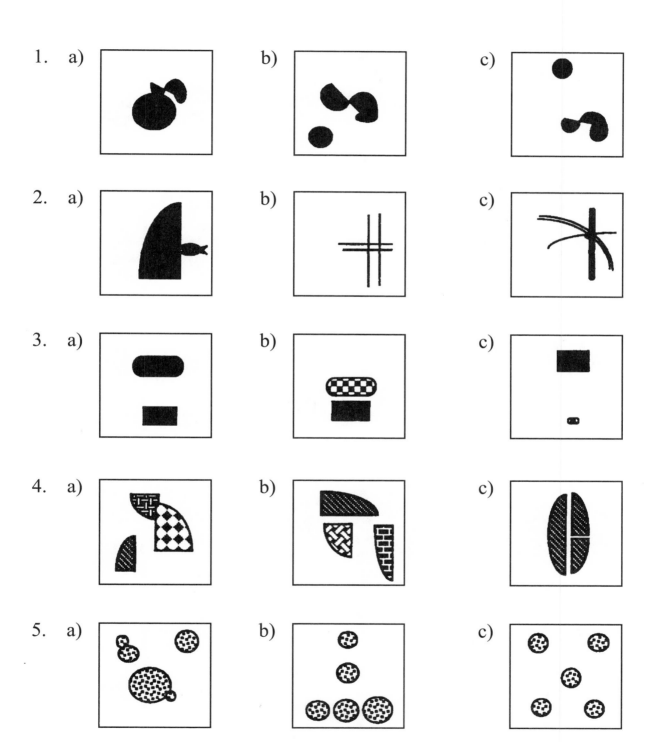

Directions: Read the following rationale for the most-artistic answers. How many of these answers had you selected?

1. a) This is the most artistically appealing choice because it has more balance than the other two and because it bears a resemblance to something most of us find visually attractive—the sight of an apple. Further interest is added through the union of the two shapes, giving the eye a focus instead of having the eye jump between the two images.

2. c) This has the most graceful lines. Straight ones are juxtaposed with curved ones in a visually pleasing way. Further, it has contrasts that draw us to the combination of lines— curved and straight, of course, but also black and white, vertical and horizontal, thick and thin.

3. b) This offers the most interesting contrast, not only in the shapes but also in the patterns of the shapes. There is also more balance in selection b) than there is in selection c).

4. c) This image is a unified one. It leaves the viewer feeling peaceful, whereas the other two create fractured, fragmented impressions.

5. a) This is the most interesting because of the use of space between the circles. The other choices are too predictable, too perfectly spaced to offer much reason for the viewer to want to dwell on them.

Overview: Participants will collaborate to express work-related ideas in kinesthetic terms.

Objective: To stimulate participants to consider alternative modes of expression.

Supplies:
- Transparency #21-1
- Overhead projector
- Flipchart

Time: About 15 minutes

Advance Preparation: Download Transparency #21-1. If possible, arrange seating so groups of four or five can work together.

Participants/Application: No matter the size of the group, this exercise will stimulate creative views on common organizational issues. Hence, it can be used at any time during the training session—as an opening, closing, or in-the-middle way of synthesizing the learning that has occurred.

Introduction to Concept:

"Synesthesia" is a cognitive power enjoyed by a rare few. The word refers to the natural and involuntary ability to simultaneously perceive stimuli with the senses usually employed and the senses not usually employed. There are people, for example, who not only see but "hear" color as it comes into their range of vision. There are those who can touch a keyboard and as they do, the "taste" of the keyboard pops into their minds automatically. A related term is "kinesthesia," which refers to the expression of an idea in atypical sensory terms. To illustrate, you cannot literally feel negative interpersonal relationships. However, if you could, would they feel to the touch like velvet or like sandpaper? If you could hear a motivated group of employees, would they sound like popcorn popping, or a pellet dropping through sludge? Kinesthesia is not only a creative means of articulating a concept, it is often a useful means. In terms of thinking skills, it ranks among the highest-order abilities, according to the taxonomy established by Dr. Benjamin Bloom: it asks us to make relationships between disparate pieces of knowledge.

Procedure:

1. Begin by recording on the flipchart either key issues facing the participants as employees or else key words they would associate with the training being conducted. Record at least 20 terms.

2. Divide the group into teams of four or five. Explain the next steps as they look at the transparency. (Show Transparency #21-1 now.)

    Once your team has selected one issue or key concept from the list on the flipchart, you will work to express that idea in kinesthetic terms.

Next, take a few minutes to list as many related terms as you can. For "popcorn," as an illustration, you might have added "oil," "butter," "salt," "Orville Reddenbacher," "kernel," "microwave," "movie theater," and so on. You should have at least ten additional words to work with.

Finally, your team will prepare a statement of one paragraph in length using both kinesthetic descriptions and the related words; it should explore the issue you have chosen and suggest a way to improve upon the existing reality or a recommended course of action.

Here's an example for you:

We hear motivation popping like popcorn all over our office. Kernels of ideas are exploding all the time. Management, of course, can add "butter" and "salt" in the form of equipment and support. But as you microwavers know, popcorn can easily burn and employees can burn out if there is no follow-through on the ideas bursting out of their mental membranes.

3. Allow about ten minutes for the groups to prepare their statements.

4. Call on a spokesperson from each team to share the kinesthetic creations with the class as a whole.

Extending the Activity:

1. Collect magazine advertisements (such as the one for luncheon meats that shows a bowling ball hitting pins) or other kinesthetic examples, such as the title of the Jack Canfield–Mark Victor Hansen book, *Chicken Soup for the Soul.* Share these with the group as examples of how powerful kinesthesia can be as an expressive force.

2. Have participants identify one problem they feel they most need help with, such as stress reduction. Then begin a collection of ideas for converting distress to eustress. Work with the group to find a fitting kinesthetic title for the collection. ("Herbal Tea for the Employee's Soul" is one example.)

3. Ask participants to list ten to twenty workplace characteristics. Then, in pairs, they will draw quick sketches in order to complete this kinesthetic prompt:

    This is what _____ does for/to _____.

    To illustrate: The sketch could be a jackhammer breaking up concrete. The sentence could read, "This is what recognition does to employees' gripes."

Workplace Connections:

1. The ever-popular Dilbert cartoon series was created around working conditions employees felt were worth writing about. Workers e-mailed their gripes to Scott Adams and the empire-builder struck back in the most charmingly comedic way possible. Somewhere in every organization is an individual with artistic ability. If participants can funnel their workplace issues/concerns/problems to him or her, the artist may be able to produce a comparable Dilbert series, with a kinesthetic title for the series; e.g., "Hot Fudge for Monday – Friday."

2. Recommend that employees keep journals (at home) of workplace anecdotes or occurrences. After the description of each, they should give it a "kinesthetic" title.

3. The next time the organization's leader makes a major address (or writes in the annual report or company newsletter), participants can be on the lookout for kinesthetic references and can discuss them with one another afterwards.

Questions for Further Consideration:

1. Why do you think the *Chicken Soup for the Soul* title has so captivated book-buyers?

2. As you think back over things you have done, seen, read, heard in your lifetime, what unusual expressions come to mind? (Albert Einstein, for example, once explained Euclidian geometry with reference to a slab of marble.)

3. How can we expand our analytic power to go beyond the literal?

4. Who in your workplace do you think would most appreciate your occasional description of a workplace issue in kinesthetic terms?

5. What might prevent you from using such a description with this person?

1. From the list of recorded ideas, select one.

2. Express it in kinesthetic terms.

3. Make a list of related terms.

4. Write a paragraph telling what needs to be done to produce improvement.

Overview: Employee morale as well as organizational climates are considerably enhanced by a singular mindset or pervasive expression that captures the organization's "irreducible essence." This activity has participants create that code/expression.

Objective: To help participants define the key focus of their team, department, or organization and to create a logo to reflect this focus.

Supplies:
- Transparency #22-1
- Overhead projector
- Headband-size strips of plain fabric or even paper and masking tape, one per participant
- Marking pens
  (The headbands and pens are optional.)

Time: 15–20 minutes

Advance Preparation: Download Transparency #22-1. Collect strips of fabric or paper, if the optional activity will be conducted, and have them available, along with marking pens for table groups of four or five. Arrange seating that best accommodates such an arrangement.

Participants/ Application: Any number of participants can engage in this exercise, which can be adapted to any stage of the training program. It works well as an icebreaker, with teams deciding the kind of learners they will be for that day. It also works well as a session-stimulator, asking participants to describe how the learning thus far acquired supports the organizational focus. It can even be used as a concluding activity, with participants creating a logo that tells how they intend to apply what they have learned.

Introduction to Concept:

On his deathbed, Senator Hubert Humphrey spoke to Reverend Jesse Jackson about "irreducible essences." When all else is stripped away, Humphrey rhetorically asked, what remains at the core of a human being? What does he or she stand for? What meaning has his or her life had? What is the fundamental, abiding, and unshakable faith he or she has held? Such questions are difficult to answer but important to consider from time to time.

We can extend the irreducible-essence question from the microcosmic to the macrocosmic perspective by asking, in reference to our own organization: What do we stand for? What defines our purpose? Who are we?

The Absolut Vodka company once asked 51 artists (one from each state and one from the District of Columbia) to capture the essence of their home state. The proceeds from the sale of the artists' lithographs went to the Design Industries Foundation for AIDS. How would you capture the essence of your state on canvas? [Pause. Elicit discussion.] The essence of your city? [Pause. Elicit discussion.] The essence of your organization? [Pause, Elicit discussion.]

Think now about the work unit or team of which you are part. Assume that the people at your table are your team members. What phrase would capture your fundamental spirit? Look at this example as you ponder. In many Asian companies, employees wear headbands bearing inspirational phrases they themselves created. This one says, "Inevitable Victory." [Show Transparency #22-1 now.]

Workplace Connections:

1. After showing the transparency, give another example. Ask, "If you were designing a headband for members of this class to wear, what phrase would you put on it?" Elicit suggestions and offer one of your own: "Open Head, Open Heart, Open Hand." (The last entry meaning participants are eager to have handouts.)

2. Have table groups of four or five design a suitable slogan for their learning experience, their workplace situation, or even their corporate identity. Encourage creativity. Tell them they are not limited to words alone. Take them through a logo-creating process by following these steps:

    a. Ask participants to think about a specific image, one that can be spatially low (a pebble in your shoe) or high (clouds with silver linings) or anywhere in between (the chasms that can only be crossed in one huge leap and not tiny, incremental steps). Allow them a few minutes to discuss and make notes about this particular prompt.

    b. Now ask the teams to think about their organization. As they do so, ask what songs come into their minds. With what specific references? Again, give them a few minutes to bounce song-related ideas around and to make notes as they do so.

    c. Next, they are to imagine the organization as a living entity, in humanoid shape, taking part in some sport. What shape would the firm have? What sport would they engage in? What movements/gestures would be used? They will share with each other what they "see" and make a few notes during these exchanges.

    d. Finally, have them review their notes and work to create a truly unusual and absolutely usable logo. The artwork need not be complicated (witness Macintosh's bitten apple). And the words need not be literary or long-winded (witness Nike's "Just do it"). But the logo (words alone or words-plus-image) should be both creative and captivating.

3. Call on a spokesperson from each team to share the team's final product.

Extending the Activity:

1. Depending on the willingness of the group to extend their verbal logos to visual ones, headbands can be created to reflect their logos. (As facilitator, you will know after an hour or so how "stiff" or serious the group is. The headband extension is recommended only for groups that seem to get along well, and/or know each other well, and/or groups in which laughter is frequently heard.) Pass out marking pens, cloth strips (or even paper strips) and masking tape so participants can make and then wear their self-styled headbands. The extension could turn into a contest, with an outsider (another facilitator, the head of Human Resources, a senior manager) as the judge.

2. Lead a brief discussion of inspirational expressions that have served us as a nation ("Remember the Maine," "Support our troops") or were used by, say, a city whose football team has made it to the playoffs ("IncrediBills" or "We're #1!")

Workplace Connections:

1. If workplace teams have not chosen names, suggest that employees create a logo instead of the usual descriptors ("The Red Team" or the "Process Action Team #2").

2. Suggest that participants read books such as Masaaki Imai's *Kaizen* that reveal the numerous ways solidarity is achieved in Japanese firms.

Questions for Further Consideration:

1. Ever since your childhood days, you have been part of organizations that characterized themselves with logos or slogans ("Semper Paratus" for Boy Scouts, for example). What are some of those from educational institutions or non-work groups to which you have belonged?

2. If you were to characterize a previous workplace, company, or department for which you worked, what would be a good logo?

3. In what other ways is unity achieved in organizations?

"Inevitable Victory"

Overview: Participants will be asked to solve the 15 puzzles that are posted around the room during morning breaks. Just before lunch, you will determine who has solved the most problems.

Objective: To stimulate creative thought about cause-specific problems and to create a structure for participants to get to know one another better.

Supplies:
- 15 blue self-adhesive circles for each two participants
- 15 sheets of 8½ x 11 typing paper
- Marking pens (ideally blue in color)
- Flipchart
- Three token prizes

Time: About 10 minutes altogether

Advance Preparation: On each of the sheets of paper, write (ideally with a blue marking pen) one of the following puzzles, and post the sheets around the room:

1) B N
2) B & B
3) B C S
4) C M M B
5) O in a B M
6) W C
7) B B M
8) B V
9) W C W
10) W E
11) W as a G
12) J W S
13) W K
14) S W
15) W C of D

Participants/ Application: This exercise works best as an opening activity. As participants enter, pair them off two-by-two, ask them to sit together as a pair, and give 15 blue self-adhesive circles to each pair. Explain that one person will write his or her name on seven of the circles and his or her partner will write his or her name on the remaining eight. If there is one person left, he or she can either join a pair to create a triad (then give five adhesive circles to each member of the triad) or can work alone (using all 15 circles). The size of the group has no bearing on the effectiveness of this icebreaker.

Introduction to Concept:

During the Carter presidency, Americans tied yellow ribbons on trees to show their support for hostages in the American Embassy in Iran. Since then, the number, types, and colors of various ribbons to show support for various causes has multiplied. What are some of them? [Pause. Elicit responses.]

If you were asked by the head of your organization to create a new ribbon design, what would it look like? What color would it be? What point would it be making or what cause would it be supporting?

Procedure:

1. Allow the pairs about five minutes to introduce themselves and then to answer these questions. Then call on a few pairs at random to share their ideas.

2. Continue with your remarks as follows:

   When you came in a short time ago, I gave each of you seven or eight circles and asked you to write your name on each. If you haven't done so yet, please do so now. [Pause.] *Now, if you'll look around the room, you'll see that I have put up fifteen sheets of paper. Each has a puzzle on it. The puzzle may look like this.* [Write "B on P" on the flipchart.] *But these puzzles, like the ribbons you just created, are related to a specific color: "blue" or "white." You have been given only the first letter of each word in the phrase. Some of the phrases are song titles or names of products. Others are common expressions.*

   For example, this "B on P" stands for "Blues on Parade." Glance around the room from time to time and answer as many puzzle questions as you can by placing a circle with your name on it on the puzzle you've solved. The trick, though, is to place the circle on the puzzle only during a natural movement around the room. So, for example, if we are taking a stretch break and your arm just happens to stretch to this puzzle [Demonstrate.], *then you could legitimately place a circle on it. Of course, if you have to leave the room to go to the restroom, you could legitimately brush your hand against a puzzle on your way out of the room.* [Demonstrate.] *Or, if we are about to take a break and you and your partner have solved five of the puzzles, you could, of course, place five circles on the puzzles like this.* [Demonstrate, moving as rapidly as you can, to increase the humorous effect.] *There will be prizes for the winning team.*

   Answers: 1–Blue Nun, 2–Black and Blue, 3–Blue Chip Stock, 4–Call Me Mr. Blue, 5–Once in a Blue Moon, 6–White Christmas, 7–Blue Bonnet Margarine, 8–Blue Velvet, 9–White Collar Worker, 10–White Elephant, 11–White as a Ghost, 12–January White Sale, 13–White Knights, 14–Snow White, 15–White Cliffs of Dover.

3. Just before lunch, ask, "Did any pair get rid of all their blue circles?" If so, award the prizes. If not, ask, "Who has just one circle left?" [That pair gets the prizes.] If no one has only one left, continue asking, "Who has just two left?" and so on until you find the winning team.

Extending the Activity:

1. You can replace the "blue" and "white" puzzles with any other color for the afternoon session. These fifteen, for example, refer to the color green.

1)	G H	(Green Hornet)
2)	G G G of H	(Green, Green Grass of Home)
3)	E G	(Emerald Green)
4)	G with E	(Green with Envy)
5)	G B	(Greenback)
6)	G T	(Green Thumb)
7)	G H	(Greenhouse)
8)	G B P	(Green Bay Packers)
9)	G P	(Green Power)
10)	G O	(Green Onion)
11)	G R	(Green Room)
12)	G T	(Green Tea)
13)	G S	(Green Snake or Green Sleeves)
14)	G P	(Greenpeace or Green Pepper)
15)	G H E	(Greenhouse Effect)

2. As a related-theme energizer later in the same training day, ask small groups to make as long a list as they possibly can of titles that contain a color reference. (For example, Alice Walker's *The Color Purple* or the song "Tie a Yellow Ribbon 'Round the Old Oak Tree.")

Workplace Connections:

1. Many people enjoy word-search challenges. Ask participants to discuss the key terms related to the work they and other department members do. Then have the participants take the words co-workers have suggested and create word-search puzzles for all to enjoy.

2. Challenge participants to create two-minute challenges for the next meeting they attend. The challenges would be general ones ("Who can come up with the longest list of titles that contain a number, such as 'Three Dog Night'?") or work-related ones ("How many words can you think of that relate to the work we do *and* that start with a 'p,' such as the word 'professional'?"). These can be used to get cerebral juices flowing prior to the start of the session.

Questions for Further Consideration:

1. How are newly hired employees made to feel welcome in your company?

2. Can you think of a way to quicken the process?

3. What do employees in your place of work do for fun?

4. If you were asked to create a monthly contest, what could you come up with?

5. How do you feel about competition in general?

Overview:	With this activity, participants have an opportunity to unscramble words and determine which does not belong in the list. After this initial challenge, they determine the key words or pegs on which instructional knowledge can be "hung" by unscrambling them.
Objective:	• To teach participants how to spot word clues and use them to gain further understanding. • To provide practice in solving verbal problems.
Supplies:	• Copies of Worksheet #24-1, one per participant • Token prizes (optional)
Time:	About 15 minutes
Advance Preparation:	Make copies of Worksheet #24-1. If you can, arrange seating so that pairs or triads can work together.
Participants/ Application:	This exercise can be adapted to any number of participants, who will work in pairs or triads. Its flexibility allows it to be used as a session-starter, a session-concluder, or as a session-stimulator.

Introduction to Concept:

Our intelligence has been tested ever since elementary school days. When we enter the Armed Forces, when we apply to college or graduate school, when we seek employment, we are being asked to solve problems that test not only how quick-witted we are but also how perceptive we are as we seek to make sense out of seemingly nonsensical situations.

Today, I have for you and your partner(s) a set of problems not unlike those that appear on intelligence tests. But don't be thrown. You will, in fact, enjoy solving these. You'll begin by unscrambling the words, four of which belong in the same category and one of which does not. If you are the first pair or triad to figure out which word in each combination is the inappropriate word, you just may win a prize today.

Procedure:

1. Distribute Worksheet #24-1. Ask the pairs/triads to inform you as soon as they have finished the entire sheet.

2. Quickly check the answers of the winning team. (The answers are 1–b (Verdi, Jabar, Schubert, Liszt, Mozart), 2–e (Warsaw, Bonn, Paris, Washington, Chrysler), 3–a (calendar, wagon, tractor, cart, carriage), 4–b (pencil, child, stapler, desktop, cabinet), 5–c (toaster, cupboard, leather, refrigerator, pantry), 6–d (tennis, fishing, football, Washington, lacrosse). Award the prizes accordingly.

3.   If you are using the exercise as a session-starter, ask the pairs to write down five key words related to their expectations for the training they are about to undertake. Next, they will scramble the letters of the words and pass the puzzles (minus the answers) to another pair (receiving theirs in return), and try to solve them.

       If the exercise is used during the session or at the end of it, the key words will be those related to the major concepts/skills they have acquired during the day.

Extending the Activity:

1.   Use phrases directly related to the topic of the training program; e.g., time management:

       m a n a g e p r i o r i t i e s (a e a m n g i i i e o s t r r p)

       l e a r n t o s a y n o (a n e r l o t a s y o n)

       k e e p a l o g (e e p k a g o l)

       a p p o i n t a t e a m l e a d e r (t p n i o p a a m t a e e e a d l r)

       h a v e a t o - d o l i s t (e a v h a o o-d t s i l t)

       The fourth entry would not directly relate to the other recommendations for managing time.

2.   Encourage participants to submit puzzles to publications that pay to publish them. Many airline magazines, for example, have a page devoted to mental challenges.

Workplace Connections:

1.   Work with the editor of the organizational newspaper to include work-related puzzles each month in the firm's publication.

2.   Ask for volunteers to form a special committee that will compile a list of questions from co-workers for which answers are hard to find. On a monthly basis, the committee will review the questions and select one they feel needs to be considered by upper management. The question may be related to an absurdity that causes employees to think, "I just can't understand why we're doing it this way." (Sam Walton understood the power of such frustration, for he encouraged Wal-Mart employees to "Eliminate the dumb.") Or the question may simply reflect the need for more information or greater clarification.

Questions for Further Consideration:

1.   Puzzles develop our concentrative ability; when we are working on them, we are aware of little else. What other kinds of exercises can develop this ability?

2.   What process did you use to figure out these answers? How does your method compare to the method used by the most successful puzzle-solver here?

Directions: Unscramble the letters to find the words. Then circle the word that does not belong in the grouping.

1. a)   R D V E I
    b)   R B J A A
    c)   T S R H C B E U
    d)   Z S L T I
    e)   Z T O R A M

2. a)   W W A A S R
    b)   N N B O
    c)   S R A P I
    d)   W N O H T G N A S I
    e)   L S H R C Y E R

3. a)   A A E R D N C L
    b)   A N G W O
    c)   R R T C A O T
    d)   R A C T
    e)   R R G I A A C E

4. a)   L N E I C P
    b)   L I D H C
    c)   R P L T S E A
    d)   P S K D T O E
    e)   T B N I E A C

5. a)   T T E A O S R
    b)   D R B P C O U A
    c)   T E E L A H R
    d)   R R R R E E F G T O A I
    e)   Y T R P N A

6. a)   N N T S I E
    b)   G H S N F I I
    c)   O O L L T A F B
    d)   G A T H W O N N I S
    e)   C S S A E O L R

Overview:	Participants will work in small groups on a number of problems that call for careful analysis. Each group will then create a checklist of steps to be taken when corporate crises occur.
Objective:	• To provide practice with problems requiring critical thinking. • To ascertain the steps involved in the "damage-control" process.
Supplies:	• Copies of Worksheet #25-1, one per participant • Overhead projector • Five or six blank transparencies • Pens for writing on transparencies
Time:	35–45 minutes
Advance Preparation:	Makes copies of Worksheet #25-1. Put tables and chairs into formations that allow four or five participants to work together.
Participants/ Application:	This exercise, which works with any number of participants, can be employed at any time during the instructional day. As an opener, it stimulates collaboration among participants and underscores the need for participants to use critical thinking throughout the training session (no matter the topic). As an energizer, it is a good change-of-pace activity, bound to reawaken interest because of its real-world familiarity. As a session-closer, it reinforces the need for participants to think analytically when they return to the workplace, where crises invariably occur.

Introduction to Concept:

The unofficial "Wizard of Spin" is Michael Sitrick, who is best known for his crisis management resolutions. If ever a situation requires critical thinking, it is when a crisis has erupted and needs to be contained. Companies that take action without analysis can put their very existence into jeopardy. Sitrick cites the case of the executive who denied a reporter's implication that the company was having trouble paying its vendors. His denial was based on truth—the company was *not* having cash flow problems. Vendors were receiving monies that were due them. However, when the story broke, the denial caused vendors to wonder if perhaps they were about to start receiving late payments. The company wound up bankrupt.

The spin doctor would have advised the executive to ask the reporter which vendors were making this claim. The executive could have then uncovered the actual problem and could have reported that to the journalist—probably the same day. In the interim, he could have given the journalist the names of dozens of other vendors who were satisfied with payment schedules.

There are many ways to report truth. But for a cynical public, the most believable truths are usually not those that claim un-truths are untrue. Today, you and your teammates will have an opportunity to play CEO-for-a-day. After specifying how you would react to each of these real-world scenarios, you will formulate a plan of action for crisis situations in general.

Procedure:

1. Distribute Worksheet #25-1. Allow 15 to 20 minutes for small groups to complete the assignment.

2. Have each small group join another small group to exchange action plans and then to prepare a composite action plan, synthesizing the best of each original. The synthesized plans will be printed on a blank transparency.

3. Have a spokesperson from each group of 8–10 present their action plans to the group at large.

4. Share with the class the fact that all of the case studies actually happened to Procter and Gamble, Chesterfield, and General Foods, and were handled with varying degree of "critical" success.

Extending the Activity:

1. Interview the CEO of the organization sponsoring the training you are presenting. Learn about crises that have arisen in the organization's history. Use these as the basis for a comparable worksheet.

2. Invite the head of a public relations firm to the class to critique the action plans the teams have created.

Workplace Connections:

1. Ask each participant, upon his or her return to work, to fashion a response to this question: "What is the worst thing that could happen here?" Next, he or she should describe the steps that would prevent the crisis or, if it is unavoidable, to outline the steps that would reduce the severity of the consequences. These plans should then be shared with upper management if comparable plans do not already exist.

2. Encourage post-class benchmarking to learn what plans other organizations have in place.

Questions for Further Consideration:

1. If the head of your organization were to do your job for just one day, what would he or she learn? What would most surprise the person?

2. How prepared do you feel your organization is for crises in the workplace?

A. Assume you are the head of a successful company that produces household products. Suddenly, you find the entire country talking about your logo, a moon with stars clustered around it. The talk has an ugly tone—people are saying the symbol represents Satan. You fear the public will lose faith in your product. On the other hand, you have worked hard to achieve that well-recognized corporate identity. What specific steps would you take to battle the rumors?

1) _____
2) _____
3) _____
4) _____
5) _____

B. It is 1934. You are CEO of a cigarette company. While you know that heavy cigarette smoking produces a bad cough in some smokers, you are certain smoking does not produce leprosy. Nonetheless, a rumor is rapidly spreading that your company in Richmond, Virginia, has employed a leper and that people who smoke the cigarettes he has touched are getting leprosy. What, specifically, would you do to counter these untruths?

1) _____
2) _____
3) _____
4) _____
5) _____

C. The new product, a carbonated candy, looked like a dream come true. Soon after its introduction, however, stories began to travel across the country that the candy exploded in the digestive system. What would you do to counter the false claims of sickness and death?

1) _____
2) _____
3) _____
4) _____
5) _____

Having considered three specific scenarios, prepare an action plan detailing what steps should be followed, generally speaking, when crises occur at your company.

1) _____
2) _____
3) _____
4) _____
5) _____

Overview: This activity presents participants with a number of problems, the solution to which requires the ability to spot trends or patterns. Extending this kind of thinking, participants will be asked to consider emerging trends in the world of business.

Objective: To strengthen analytical skills.

Supplies:
- Transparency #26-1
- Overhead projector
- Flipchart
- Token prize (optional)

Time: About 25 minutes

Advance Preparation: Purchase a small prize if you have decided to use such. Download the transparency. Write the two examples from the Introduction on the flipchart but keep them covered until they are needed.

a) 1 10 3 9 5 8 7 9 6 ___ ___
b) 8 10 36 92 256 696 ___

Arrange seating, if the room permits, so table groups of four or five can work together.

Participants/ Application: The best times to use this exercise with groups are at the beginning of the training session and at the end. As a warm-up, it enables small groups of participants to start working as a team from the very start of the class. It also establishes the context within which they will be working: in a challenging environment that requires them to do more than just sit passively and absorb information. In such a context, participants are expected to think about what they are learning and to form their own frames of reference.

As a concluding exercise, the problems posed and the discussion prompted by them work to encourage thought about the future. For the immediate future, you can ask how participants will apply the training. For the more distant future, you can ask participants to consider the megatrends that futurists claim are already beginning to emerge.

Introduction to Concept:

Futurists John Naisbitt and Patricia Aburdene encourage us to think about the information we receive on a daily basis and what it is really telling us. To learn what it is really telling us means we must spot and carefully analyze the trends that seem to be emerging. Critical thinking of this type requires time, comparison, and lots of questions. If we are unwilling to engage in such thought-provocative action, however, we may truly find ourselves shocked by the future.

Engaging in simple pursuits often allows us to establish the framework within which more complicated analysis can occur. Developing the ability to discern patterns sharpens the skills of analysis and can lead to valuable insights, such as identification of emerging trends. An example of a small-scale analysis task is this. [Show these examples, written on the flipchart, one at a time.] Ask participants to guess what numbers come next in the series.

a) 1 10 3 9 5 8 7 7 9 6 ___ ___

b) 8 10 36 92 256 696 ___

Procedure:

1. After a few minutes, if participants still have not figured out the problems on the flipchart, share the answers. They are: a) **11** (because the odd numbers are increasing by 2 each time), and **5** (because the even number, 10, goes down by one each time) and b) **1904**, because two numbers are added together each time (8 + 10 = 18) and then multiplied by 2 to obtain the next number in the series (36). Next, 36 is added to 10, to obtain 46, which is then doubled to obtain 92, and so on.

2. Offer a token prize to the first participant who is able to repeat this sequence (or write it on the board) without referring to notes. [Allow enough time for at least one person to come to the front of the room to try writing the sequence from memory.]

105, 989, 184, 777, 063, 564, 942, 352, 821, 147

Most participants will set right to work attempting to memorize the numbers, when in fact there is a very powerful gimmick operating here: the numbers are organized in increments of seven. So all one really needs to do is remember where to end: at 105. Starting with 7 and adding seven each time will ultimately lead the token-prize winner to 105 (989, 184, 777, 063, 564, 942, 352, 821, 147).

Point out that data and information are not always organized so neatly for us, but when they are, we are able to recall the information more quickly and more successfully.

3. Show Transparency #26-1, noting that patterns are sometimes buried among numbers, sometimes among words, and sometimes by events themselves. Have groups of five or six participants work on the transparency problems, the answers to which are:

    1) The next letter is "N," continuing the spelling out of the numbers from 1 to 9.

    2) Share the answer: The numbers, if written as words, are alphabetically arranged. Then discuss the need to go beyond the obvious, to move outside the box as we problem-solve.

    3) Christmas, because there is no "I." [Noel]

4) The same groups will then work to describe at least three trends they believe are emerging in their field, industry, world of business, or the economy itself. They should, whenever possible, back up their opinions with statistics.

5) After 10 or 15 minutes, merge two groups and have them share the trends they have "spotted" with each other.

6) Following this discussion, call on one spokesperson from each merged group to share the essence of their predictions.

7) Conclude the activity by encouraging participants to form their own frames of reference, based on carefully assimilated information and carefully constructed patterns. Acknowledge that these reference-points may have to be calibrated from time to time.

Extending the Activity:

1. Sometimes misunderstanding prevents us from solving problems. Here is one example:

   In a good-sized metropolis of 350,488 citizens, 7% of the people in the greater metropolitan area have unlisted phone numbers. One night, as you thumb through the phone book, you choose three pages at random (containing a total of 900 names). How many of those will have unlisted numbers?

   The answer, of course, is zero, because if they are not listed, they will not be in the phone book in the first place. Invite participants to share other examples of times when misunderstanding caused problems to be created or to remain unsolved.

2. Use the stratification device to discern what patterns may be emerging among workplace issues; have participants quickly list 20 to 30 problems or concerns that come to mind when they think about work. Then have them analyze the list to find patterns, trends, or clusters.

Workplace Connections:

1. Suggest that employees meet on a regular basis to make predictions for the next three, six, and twelve months about their workplace, technology, and general trends in their business world, after the course concludes. Then encourage them to meet on the anniversary dates three, six, and twelve months later to learn whose predictions had the greatest accuracy. That person, perhaps, can be awarded the money others have put into a "prediction" pot.

2. Recommend that participants continue developing their trend-spotting skills by reading *Megatrends 2000* or a similar future-oriented book. They should discuss the ideas presented and the ideas they come up with with at least one other person in the workplace.

Questions for Further Consideration:

1. What trends do you feel are emerging in terms of medical advances?

2. What trends do you believe are emerging in terms of our lifestyles?

3. What trends do you see emerging as far as the makeup of the workforce is concerned?

4. What trends do you foresee occurring in terms of technology?

5. What preparations is your organization making to be ready for these changes?

What comes next?

1) O T T F F S S E _____

What's the pattern in this arrangement?

2) 86 11 4 90 1 7 16 12 28 2 _____

What's the holiday?

3) A B C D E F G H I J K M N O
P Q R S T U V W X Y Z

Overview:	Participants will begin by studying the Triple-A Approach and then using it to formulate a persuasive proposal on a workplace issue. The presentation will be evaluated by other class members.
Objective:	To familiarize participants with the Triple-A Approach to presenting information.
Supplies:	• Transparency #27-1 • Overhead projector • Scraps of paper
Time:	Approximately 30 minutes
Advance Preparation:	Download the transparency. Cut up scraps of paper, six or seven for each participant.
Participants/ Application:	Arrange for table groups of five or six to work together. This exercise works well as a session-opener (to illustrate that in training-session teams or on workplace teams or simply in everyday encounters, persuasion skills are indeed valuable) or as a change-of-pace activity that asks participants to critique what was learned thus far and to persuade others to accept their opinions regarding which elements of the instructional content are likely to have most relevance in the workplace.

Introduction to Concept:

Author Ken Blanchard asserts that "the key to successful leadership today is influence, not authority." We influence others by our example, to be sure, but also by our words—whether those words are delivered by speaking, by writing, or by the electronic medium. Sometimes, when we observe others who always seem to get what they want, we are envious or puzzled by the apparent magic they exert over others. In truth, though, the persuaders we admire have finely tuned their communication skills.

One tool that will assist you in your effort to make a point and influence others to accept your viewpoint is the Triple-A Approach. It focuses on three factors. [Show Transparency #27-1 now and briefly discuss the elements.]

Procedure:

1. Once participants have had a chance to review the transparency, divide the class into groups of five or six.

2. Assign each group one of the following topics to be developed using the Triple-A Approach. (You may choose other topics that may have special relevance for your participants. Or, if the activity is used as a concluding activity, the different groups will try to persuade others to adopt their point of view regarding which aspects of the training session were the most valuable.)

   We should have a dress code at work.

   > Mondays and Fridays should be "dress-down days."

   > Secretaries should receive a percentage of their boss's annual bonus.

   > Employees should be able to evaluate their supervisors.

   > Employees should be allowed to use the Internet for personal business during slow periods.

3. Allow the teams about 20 minutes to write out their arguments and to select a spokesperson to deliver the written remarks.

4. Before or after the spokesperson attempts to persuade the other groups, distribute small sheets of paper. Upon the conclusion of each presentation, ask participants (other than members of the presenting group) to write one word on their papers: "Yes" (indicating the argument was persuasive) or "No" (indicating the argument did not influence their thinking).

5. Collect the scraps and pass them to the presenting group.

Extending the Activity:

1. Show a videotape of a well-known persuasive speech (such as the President's State of the Union address or a lawyer's closing argument) and analyze it as a group, using the factors in the Triple-A Approach as the criteria.

2. Invite the top salesperson from a local real estate firm to address the class on the reasons for his or her success in selling.

3. Ask small groups to create an acronym of their own for decision-making.

Workplace Connections:

1. Request that participants identify one individual in their workplace having the toughest decision of all to make. Then recommend that they meet with that person to learn more about the process of decision-making. Suggest that they make notes on the meeting, to be shared with the individual first and later with groups of employees.

2. Employees should reflect weekly on the percentage of time they spent at work absorbing knowledge, the percentage of time they spent developing new ideas, the percentage of time they spent implementing those ideas, and the percentage of time spent evaluating new ideas. A simple graphic will enable them to tell at a glance if they are maintaining a roughly equal division among the categories, such as this one:

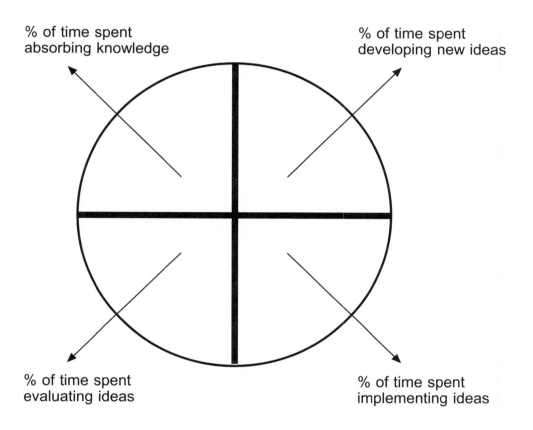

% of time spent
absorbing knowledge

% of time spent
developing new ideas

% of time spent
evaluating ideas

% of time spent
implementing ideas

Questions for Further Consideration:

1. How much discussion is typically accorded decisions made in your workplace?

2. To what extent are employees invited to voice their opinions?

3. What factors do you take into account as you make decisions at work?

4. In terms of organizational or national history, what poor decisions can you recall prominent people having made? What elements went into the poor decision-making?

5. What works well in preventing "groupthink" from occurring?

Appeal

- to their emotions
- to their WIFM need
  (What's in it for me?)
- to their basic sense of
  decency/fairness

Anticipate

- their questions
- their objections
- their reactions

Ask

- for what you need
- for commitment
- for a chance to succeed

Overview:	Participants will work with one or two others to figure out the answers to deceptively simple problems, designed to "fool" participants who do not analyze the questions carefully enough.
Objective:	To encourage participants to apply deliberate, critical thought to problem scenarios.
Supplies:	• Copies of Worksheet #28-1, one per participant • Copies of Worksheet #28-2, one per participant
Time:	About 20 minutes
Advance Preparation:	Prepare copies of the worksheets. Ideally, you can arrange seating so participants can work in pairs or triads.
Participants/ Application:	The questions on this worksheet activity are designed to fool the problem solver, in that the answers are not obvious but are definitely solvable. Any number of participants can work on this activity.

Introduction to Concept:

"There's this faculty in the human mind that hates any question that takes more than ten seconds to answer," author Norman Mailer once observed. We humans, especially we Americans, like to move. We like fast cars, time-saving machinery, and labor-saving devices. But when it comes to problems, we often move too fast, failing to give the situation the attention it deserves. Some problems, it is true, can be solved quickly. The majority, however, demand critical analysis rather than guesses. They ask problem-solvers to shift paradigms, to put assumptions aside, to deal in facts rather than conjecture.

The activity in which you will be engaged today has a number of problems for you. They are all solvable. However, they will take more than ten seconds to answer.

Procedure:

1. Distribute Worksheet #28-1 and allow about 10 minutes for completion.

2. Share the answers with participants:

    1) It may have been the apple, although there really is no evidence to suggest it was. The Bible simply refers to the fruit of "the tree of the knowledge of good and evil."

    2) Karloff played the monster created by Dr. Frankenstein.

    3) Leslie is Anthony's son.

4) The rearrangement of the matchsticks spells the word "nil," which, of course, means "nothing."

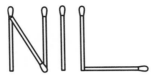

5) There were six managers representing four different professional organizations.

6) The answer is "G-I ants."

7) The answer is 28. (To help participants understand how the answer was arrived at, ask them to imagine the team members standing side by side. Team member A shakes hands with B, C, D, E, F, G, and H. That's a total of seven handshakes in the first round, because team member A is not shaking hands with himself. Then it is time for team member B. Remember, she has already shaken with A, so she shakes with C, D, E, F, G, and H, for a total of 6. Add the 7 and the 6 and you have 13 so far. Continue this way and you will get the final total of 28.)

8) Portland Trailblazers.

9) Skiing would be the penultimate experience. "Penultimate" means "next-to-the-last."

3. Distribute Worksheet #28-2 and allow a few minutes for participants to solve the mystery. (The reason Joe Saturday suspects Janice is that if Veronica had come home after Janice, Veronica's raincoat would have been on top, not Janice's.)

4. Wrap up the activity by leading a discussion regarding the kinds of things in the workday and workplace that are seen but overlooked and that could spell disaster if not attended to. Point out that Quality-meister Dr. Joseph Juran claims that American workers are so busy fighting fires that they no longer hear the alarm signals going off. Ask whether there are any alarm signals being set off in the workplace that we have been ignoring. Tie the question to events or people on the national scene who are sending out signals that we are ignoring.

Extending the Activity:

1. Have participants create a workplace mystery story of their own, in which an important clue is presented but not emphasized. The stories might center on a common problem a team is facing, for example, or a challenge with which a whole department is coping. They can exchange their stories and see how good the others were at analyzing the clues to solve the mystery.

2. Encourage a discussion of unexplained phenomena in the natural world often presented in television programs or videos ("Mysteries of the Seas," "Mysteries of the Universe," "Mysteries from the Animal Kingdom"), and puzzling events in the business world as well. ("How does the European Commonwealth function as well as it does?")

Workplace Connections:

1. Recommend that a group of participants work as fund-raising volunteers to design a murder-mystery evening with employee-actors interacting with employee-guests.

2. Rent classic murder mystery movies, such as *Dial 'M' for Murder,* and show them over a several-day period at lunchtime. Ask for a volunteer to "moderate"—i.e., stopping the video at certain points to discuss the clues spotted up to that point.

Questions for Further Consideration:

1. What specific elements go into the creation of a good "whodunit"?

2. What mysteries have recently been solved in your workplace?

3. What mysteries still remain?

4. How can organizations tap into the pleasure employees find in reading a good mystery outside of work in order to generate excitement in solving a problem at work?

5. Is your own mystery-solving style a deductive or inductive one?

Directions: Working with one or two others, you will now have an opportunity to test your critical-thinking skills—especially your analytical skills—with these questions. Read them carefully, discuss them, and then write your answer in the blank space.

1.   What fruit caused Adam and Eve to be banished from the Garden of Eden? _____

2.   Boris Karloff is known around the world for his masterful portrayal of an abnormal character in the movies. What was the name of that character? _____

3.   Assume that Leslie is a man. If Anthony's son is Leslie's father, what relationship is Leslie to Anthony? _____

4.   How can you move only two matches so that you leave nothing in this existing row of six matches?

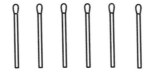

5.   A group of managers, fully aware of the importance of networking, shared the following facts with each other:

   •   Each man belongs to exactly two professional organizations.
   •   Each organization is represented in the group by exactly three managers.
   •   Every possible pair of professional organizations has exactly one member of the group in common.

   How many managers are there in the group and how many different professional organizations are represented?

6.   Combining a common verbal reference used to describe solders with a common bug, can you come up with the name of a National Football League team?

7.   There are eight team members in a warehouse. Each shakes hands just once with each of the other members of the same team. What is the total number of handshakes?

8.   Can you figure out which team in the National Basketball Association is represented by this sesquipedalian sequence: "Pathway pyromaniacs from a left-sided land"?

9.   Joe has been daydreaming of ways to spend his upcoming vacation. Among his choices are scuba-diving, horseback riding, roller-skating along Muscle Beach, visiting relatives, attending a series of baseball games, skiing, and swimming in the Pacific. The choices are arranged in ascending order of preference. Knowing this, what would you say Joe regards as the penultimate experience?

Directions: Work with one or two others to solve the mystery presented here. All the clues you need are contained in the story.

Two newly hired customer service representatives have decided to room together. Things have been going well, both on the job and in their personal lives. But approximately two months after the two women moved in together, a tragedy occurred. Detective Joe Saturday was called to the scene in response to a 9-1-1 call at about six in the morning. Here's what happened when he got to the scene.

Janice Huerrerra, visibly shaken, let the detective in. Her roommate, Veronica Barclay, lay on the floor, a long-handled knife protruding from her chest. When the detective examined the body, he found that Veronica had been dead for several hours. He gave the apartment a cursory inspection, knowing the forensic technicians were on their way. He saw a knife missing from a rack of kitchen knives, bloody towels on the bathroom floor, and two raincoats on a chair. The top one had a .38 caliber gun sticking out of the pocket.

Before he could even ask about it, Janice admitted that the gun belonged to her but claimed she had a permit for it. Saturday then asked Janice about the events that led to her phone call to 9-1-1. She explained that she had been out on a date and returned about 10:30 p.m. She went right to bed after finding a note from her roommate saying she would not be in until 1:00 a.m. or 2:00 a.m.

The next thing she remembered was hearing Veronica come in, complaining about the rainstorms. She vaguely recalled hearing Veronica throw her raincoat on a chair and whisper to someone Janice assumed was her boyfriend. Then she heard Veronica in the bathroom. Just before she dozed off again, Janice heard Veronica's bedroom door close. She is certain, however, that she heard a man's laughter coming from Veronica's bedroom.

When Janice arose early the next morning, she found the body on the floor. In response to the detective's question, she assures him that she has not touched a thing, other than the phone to call 9-1-1.

The detective decides Janice is a suspect. On what basis? _____

_____

_____

Overview: After a brief presentation of commonly used patterns, participants will work in pairs to prepare a written response to a given prompt, employing one organizational pattern.

Objective:
- To familiarize participants with the various organizational patterns that help in the assimilation and presentation of information.
- To give participants the opportunity to structure information around a specific pattern.

Supplies:
- Transparency #29-1
- Overhead projector

Time: About 20 minutes

Advance Preparation: Download Transparency #29-1. If possible, arrange the seating so pairs can work together.

Participants/ Application: This exercise, which can be used with any size group, works well as an introductory or warm-up technique, affording participants the chance to learn about each other, each other's organizations, and the use of suitable patterns for presenting what they have learned. Ideally, the pairs will be composed of participants who do not know each other well, in which case they can discuss their respective departments or organizations, and then select one to write about. If they do know each other and/or if they are from the same organization, there will be more time spent on the writing than on the getting-to-know-you information.

Introduction to Concept:

How do we find the structure or framework that allows us to organize our thoughts in a meaningful way? The process of critically studying the materials to be presented leads us to the most suitable structure among many possible structures. There is seldom a singular "right" format for ordering our thoughts. Rather, the more familiar we are with the wide array of possibilities, the more likely we are to select the one that will work best given a number of circumstances (the background of the listening or reading audience; the desired length of the presentation or document; the purpose for which you are assembling information, etc.).

Let's say you have to write an article for a business journal or teach an in-house course on the topic of management. How would you organize the information you wanted to present? You could choose one of the following: [Show Transparency #29-1 now.]

The Chronological Approach—This uses references to time. So, you might trace the evolution of various buzz words that characterized various management theories over the years, or you might discuss the historical events that came before what we are experiencing today.

The FDP (Famous Dead Persons) Approach—This uses the thoughts of industry giants as the organizing structure. You might take, for instance, Dr. Deming's Seven Deadly Sins and use them as the basis for your remarks.

The FLP (Famous Living Persons) Approach—This uses the philosophies of one or more figures known to the audience. The person(s) may be organization- or industry-specific, as opposed to international figures, but his or her influence would serve as the basis for organizing your information.

The Problem-Solution Approach—Divided into two components, this is the most popular approach used in the business world today. Basically, it begins by delineating the problem and the possible ramifications that would ensue if the problem were not solved. The briefing or report would then go on to suggest several possible solutions and would conclude with a recommendation for corrective action.

The Order-of-Importance Approach—This approach discusses several related ideas and presents them in the order the speaker or writer has deemed most important. To illustrate, if you were discussing the benefits of the "open-book management" style, you would begin with the most salient points first. (Some people prefer to "build up" to an impressive conclusion and so they do the reverse: they begin with the least significant details.)

The Deductive Approach—This begins with the premise or viewpoint or theory the presenter-of-information would like to focus on. The presenter would then proceed, quite literally, to *lead* the audience *from* this viewpoint into an understanding of the elements that constitute it.

The Inductive Approach—This is the reverse of the Deductive Approach. When we induce our audience, we literally *lead* them *into* our way of thinking through a deliberate argument that, we hope, builds to a convincing crescendo. If you wanted to prove that the current management gurus were simply "witch doctors," you would point out fallacies or weaknesses in their advice and conclude by calling them imposters.

The Topical Approach—This approach divides the topic into several components, none of which is more important than any of the others. If your topic, for instance, were "management," you could break that broad topic down into a number of components: management styles or management gurus, or changes facing managers, and so on.

There are many other ways to organize information, but these make the most frequent appearance in the world of business.

Procedure:

1. Show Transparency #29-1 and keep it visible as you discuss the examples and also while participants are working on the assignment.

2. Ask them to pair up and choose one pattern of organization around which they will organize their thoughts in response to this prompt: "Tell me about your company (or agency, installation, firm, government unit, or organization represented by attendees)."

3. Allow about five minutes for selection of a pattern and for brainstorming.

4. Then ask participants to write a one- or two-paragraph essay telling about their company from the perspective of the pattern they have chosen.

5. After 15 or 20 minutes, call on a few pairs at random to share their essays. They could either identify the pattern they have selected or they could read the essay and then ask the class to tell what the pattern was.

Extending the Activity:

1. Halfway through the course, ask the class to summarize what they have learned, using one of the patterns provided.

2. Obtain copies of actual workplace documents and have participants analyze them to determine which pattern was used.

Workplace Connections:

1. Advise participants, if they have not already done so, to learn what organizational pattern their supervisors prefer to see in the reports they prepare. While problem-solution is the most frequently used in the world of business, varying circumstances may lead to varying preferences on the part of their supervisors.

2. Encourage participants to write the name of the pattern they are using at the top of draft copies of reports. When they see the pattern, they will be reminded of the kind of information to include and what information will be superfluous. Identifying the pattern in advance means the job of analysis is cut in half, for the structure virtually dictates the inclusions.

3. Suggest that participants try to determine what pattern was used the next time they listen to a speech by someone inside or outside the organization. Have them critically assess the effectiveness of this particular pattern. If it failed somehow, encourage participants to think about the pattern they would have used instead.

4. Collect a file full of magazine articles related to the topic of the training session or to subjects that are important to participants. Distribute one article to each participant and ask them to ascertain the pattern used in the article.

Questions for Further Consideration:

1. Are you consciously aware of using patterns as you do your writing at work? Why or why not?

2. Do you spend much time revising the structure of your business documents or presentations you have to make? If so, how could the use of patterns help?

3. What additional patterns of organization are useful to business writers?

4. Think about the best speech you have ever heard. What pattern was used?

Approaches to Organizing Information

Chronological

FDP (Famous Dead Persons)

FLP (Famous Living Persons)

Problem-Solution

Order of Importance

Deductive

Inductive

Topical

Overview:	Participants will first learn how to use this simple analytical tool and then apply it to given issues that affect us as corporate and community citizens.
Objective:	To encourage careful and deliberate scrutiny of issues prior to making decisions regarding them.
Supplies:	• Transparency #30-1 • Overhead projector • Flipcharts
Time:	Approximately 15 minutes
Advance Preparation:	Download Transparency #30-1. If the training room allows flexible seating, arrange table groups of seven or eight.
Participants/ Application:	Any number of participants can use this technique, for any number of issues that arise—either during the course of the training or afterwards in team and staff meetings. If used as a session-opener, the exercise will stimulate lively discussion among participants and so will quickly break the ice that exists among strangers. If used as a concluding activity, the exercise can focus on burning issues that arose during the training program.

Introduction to Concept:

When we think in a productive fashion, we are able to generalize solutions employed in comparable situations. (Reproductive thinking, by contrast, is merely learning or memorizing correct responses without being able to extend them to similar problems.) Superficial decision-making falls more into the reproductive category than the productive, for it is almost a rote response as opposed to a carefully considered response. [Show Transparency #30-1.] There are numerous techniques that encourage thinking that goes beneath the surface. One such as the Pro Con'D model, which asks the problem-solver to consider:

Pro	—	What are the advantages to this particular issue?
Con	—	What disadvantages are associated with this issue?
'D	—	What needs to be discussed further?

For example, if I asked, "How many of you think the minimum wage should be raised?" most of you would assert that indeed it should be raised. You would probably be able to cite advantages quite readily. Now let me ask, "Would you still want to raise it if I told you that research shows the drop-out rate increases when the minimum wage is increased?"

The Pro Con'D approach puts a halt on our typical and understandable rush to judgment. It forces us to weigh the various consequences that might result from a decision that initially seems quite appealing.

Procedure:

1. Divide the class into teams of six or seven members. Appoint a team leader for each team, whose job will be to ensure that the question has been put to Pro Con'D scrutiny before the "majority-rules" answer ("yes" or "no") is given.

2. Assign each team one of the following questions (or comparable ones of your own):

    1) Should we increase the minimum wage by $2.00?

    2) Should we prevent prisoners from filing frivolous lawsuits?

    3) Should there be guarantees given when employees are hired? (If so, what should they be?)

    4) Should judges instead of juries decide the outcomes of lawsuits?

    5) Should organization heads spend more time "walking the talk"?

    6) Should the word "secretary" be replaced with something else?

    7) Should juveniles committing adult crimes be tried as adults?

    8) Should there be a cap on athletes' salaries?

    9) Should there be mandatory training for all supervisors? (If so, what should it consist of?)

    10) Should there be a cap on the salaries of CEOs?

    11) Should our organization institute a "pay-for-knowledge" system?

    12) Should team leaders receive monetary compensation?

3. Allow 10 to 15 minutes for the Pro Con'D assessment of the issue.

4. Call on each group to share the answers they arrived at after the Pro Con'D discussion.

Extending the Activity:

1. Record issues on a flipchart as they arise throughout the training program. Periodically, use the Pro Con'D tool as a format for discussion prior to deciding on a feasible course of action.

2. Scan the newspaper for several days prior to the training program. Write the issues being debated on 3" x 5" cards—enough issues so each participant can have one. Have partici-pants select a card, subject the issue to the Pro Con'D technique, and then discuss the issue with a partner, who will then share his or her Pro Con'D views on a different issue with the first person.

Workplace Connections:

1. There are "hot" topics in every workplace. Before you conclude the session, ask participants to write down five issues currently being debated at work. Then ask that they apply the Pro Con'D approach to these issues when they have time for reflection. After culling their own ideas, they should then engage others in a consideration of the issues before decisions are made about them.

2. Suggest that participants contact an arbitrator to learn how he or she is able to bring balance and equanimity of thought to situations that parties feel very strongly about.

Questions for Further Consideration:

1. How can we separate emotions from facts?

2. What has caused some of the arguments that have erupted in your workplace during the last six months?

3. What is the worst decision you ever made?

4. What factors surrounded the making of it?

5. As you reflect upon organizational decisions to proceed in one way or another, do you feel the evidence was given sufficient weight? Explain.

| Pro |

— What are the advantages to this particular issue?

| Con |

— What disadvantages are associated with this issue?

| 'D |

— What needs to be discussed further?

Overview:	Separated physically as well as by task, participants will write directions for their partners to follow. The directions ask them to draw a geometric design.
Objective:	To foster analysis of a task and to determine the best way of directing others to perform that task.
Supplies:	Handout #31-1 A for half the participants and B for the remaining half
Time:	25 minutes
Advance Preparation:	Make copies of Handout #31-1 (half the number as the number of participants) and cut in half. The two halves of the room will work on two separate assignments. Seating should be arranged for this division.
Participants/ Application:	This exercise will work with any number of participants. It is an excellent warm-up activity, but is also helpful when there has been a miscommunication between or among participants or between participants and facilitator. As a session-stimulator, it could be presented via a compliment: "You have managed to follow all the instructions I've presented thus far. However, I have been presenting instructions for a number of years. Let's see how well you can present instructions to a partner."

Introduction to Concept:

Following directions is easy if the person giving the directions has engaged in task-analysis first. Far too often, however, those who give instructions have not given thought to the best way of sharing knowledge. They have not planned in advance the most logical way to present important information.

Part of the "logic" associated with giving directions is the realization that there are numerous kinds of intelligence and numerous ways of absorbing information. Howard Gardner lists eight kinds—linguistic, logical, musical, spatial, kinesthetic, intrapersonal, interpersonal, and natural. J. P. Guilford has actually identified 124 separate and distinct kinds of intelligence; he regards them as a divisible cube of intellect.

The most efficient directions-giver appeals to the appropriate intelligence. If the intelligence is not known or if the audience has a combination of intelligences, the direction-giver appeals to more than one kind.

Procedure:

1. Physically arrange the room so that participants are sitting in one half of the room or the other. (If you do not have an even number of participants, the one "odd person out" will serve as the observer and will "float" around the room to make note of how this organization exercise was executed. The observer will make a report after the partners have conferred.)

2. Emphasize again the need to appeal to various modalities. Stress the fact that our backgrounds and experiences are different and while one person may recall geometric terms, for example, another may be thinking in terms of pies and pound cakes. And so, as good communicators, we need to express a given concept in more than one way.

3. Explain the task in the following manner: "Soon, I am going to give each of you a diagram. It is important not to let someone on the other side of the room see what you have. You are going to follow the instruction on the diagram, which essentially asks you to describe it in writing. There are certain words you cannot use."

4. Distribute Handout #31-1A to the left-hand side of the room and Handout #31-1B to the right-hand side of the room and give participants about 20 minutes to complete their written directions. They will use another sheet of paper, at the top of which they will have written their names.

5. Once they are finished, collect all the handouts, keeping the two piles separate.

6. Every person on the left-hand side will give his or her paper to a partner seated on the right-hand side and will receive a paper in return.

7. Class members will now draw a diagram based on the written instructions they were given.

8. When they are ready, you will ask the partners to sit together and to show each other their diagrams. As they do this, you will quickly give both handouts to each set of partners.

9. Give them an opportunity to compare their products to the original diagrams, stressing that the drawings should match the original exactly, including the thickness of lines and the size of the objects. Then ask each pair to decide what one thing in the directions would have improved the quality of the final product.

10. Call on each pair to share their improvement ideas as you compile a master list on chart paper.

Extending the Activity:

1. Have participants identify the criteria that constitute excellence in the giving of directions.

2. Work with them to prepare an assessment form incorporating those criteria, to be used to critique those who give instructions inside and outside the classroom.

Workplace Connections:

1. Encourage participants to "check for understanding" whenever they are given directions for completing a task that is new, difficult, or unclear to them. One of the simplest techniques they can employ is simply to paraphrase to the direction-giver their understanding of what they are to do.

2. The steps involved in the most important workplace processes should be made uniform and put into a procedural manual so that new hires or temporary replacements can work with little variation in the established processes.

Questions for Further Consideration:

1. What are some of the barriers to the effective exchange of instructions?

2. What do you think General George S. Patton meant when he said leaders should "give direction, not directions"?

3. What is the worst mistake you ever made as a result of unclear directions?

4. What would have prevented the mistake from occurring at all?

5. From whom in your lifetime have you learned the most? What made that person such an extraordinary teacher?

A. Study the following diagram carefully, because your goal is to have another person reproduce it exactly. You cannot show it to that person. Nor can you use your hands—use only your words to describe it. (You will describe it in writing and your paper will then be turned over to your partner, who will try to reproduce what you were looking at, using only the directions you gave on paper.) One more rule: As you tell your partner how to draw this illustration, you **CANNOT USE** the words "circle" or "round" or "triangle." Good luck!

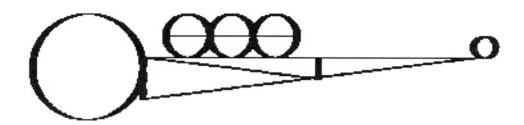

B. Study the following diagram carefully, because your goal is to have another person reproduce it exactly. You cannot show it to that person. Nor can you use your hands—use only your words to describe it. (You will describe it in writing and your paper will then be turned over to your partner, who will try to reproduce what you were looking at, using only the directions you gave on paper.) One more rule: As you tell your partner how to draw this illustration, you **CANNOT USE** the words "circle" or "round" or "triangle." Good luck!

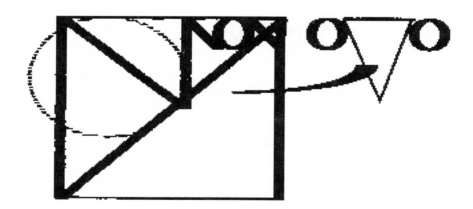

Overview: Starting with a problem best solved by actually envisioning the situations, participants will proceed to contemplate a work-related problem in the same fashion.

Objective: To foster imaginative reasoning.

Supplies: A "back-up" problem—in case some class members have seen the original sock problem before. This will suffice:

> *You have six matches and must form four equal-sided triangles from them.*

When you are tutoring the "imagine" group, encourage them to think in three dimensions, not two. If they can, they will have a flat triangle and in the space above it, three intersecting matches meeting to make three additional triangles.

Time: Approximately 20 minutes

Advance Preparation: If possible, arrange for a breakout room so that half the class can work with you in solving a problem and the other half can leave the room to work on the same problem collectively or individually.

Participants/ Application: This exercise, suitable for any number of participants, works especially well as an ice-breaker, forcing communal effort and collegiality. It can also serve as a preview to the many times during the training to follow that participants will need to engage in this sort of reasoning as various issues are addressed.

The exercise can also be used as a summarizing activity: have pairs imagine what it will be like when they return to their work sites. They can then formulate an action plan that will enable them to apply the learning they have acquired to the all-too-real circumstances awaiting them.

Introduction to Concept:

Einstein as a child used to imagine himself chasing sunbeams through space. He often spoke of the importance of fantasizing. He regarded imagination, in fact, as being "more important than knowledge." In more contemporary terms, management expert Tom Peters refers to imagination as "the only source of real value in the new economy." In the following example, the answer will come more easily if you can actually imagine yourself performing the action.

> *You have just put a load of socks into the clothes dryer. There are 16 black socks and 10 brown socks inside the dryer. Without actually looking at what you are pulling out, how many socks will you have to take out of the dryer before you have a pair that matches?*

Procedure:

1. Divide the class in half but assure participants that both teams are working on the same problem.

2. Gather one group around you and explain that you are not going to tell them the answer, but you are going to suggest that they try to find that answer by imaging themselves actually pulling socks out of the dryer, one at a time. How many socks would they need before finding a matched pair?

3. Review the answers with participants and encourage them to describe the process (if any) they used to solve the problem. Discuss how visualization could have helped (for example: You've bent over and pulled out a sock, but you cannot look at it. What color could it be? (Brown or Black.) Now you bend down and pull out another. What color is this one? (Brown or Black.) Pull out one more sock. What color is this? (Brown or Black.) What possibilities now exist with the three socks you have before you? (All three brown or all three black or two black and one brown or two brown and one black.) No matter the scenario, if you have three, you will have a matching pair.

4. Now divide the class into teams of four or five. Ask each team to select some change they are currently facing or would like to introduce (preferably work-related). Another option is for them to consider some danger or crisis situation in the workplace. Have them visualize, step-by-step, the events that could lead to various possible outcomes. Then have them re-trace those steps, specifying how they would prepare for such crisis-possibilities.

5. Call on one person from each team to share the group's imaginative reasoning.

Extending the Activity:

1. To develop spatial reasoning via visualization, prepare a number of exercises like this one:

    What will this figure look like if it is rotated or turned over? Encourage visualization to find the answer.

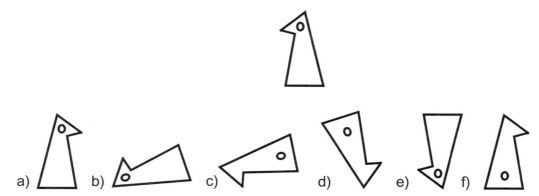

    The answer is b) (rotated) and if you wish to make it really difficult, the answer for turned over and upside-down is e).

2.   The gift of fantasy, which Einstein also valued, can work for any of us. The fantasizing process would be as simple as imagining the perfect workplace, the perfect job, the perfect friendship, etc., specifying the elements that create the perfection, and then working to achieve some or all of them. Lead participants through such a process in relation to a situation that parallels one of the most serious discussions that arose during the training day.

Workplace Connections:

1.   Encourage employees to continue their imaginative reasoning after the training is over. Using the buddy system, they can each prepare visual challenges like the first one in the extended activity. Then, on a daily basis, they can exchange their ten with those prepared by another employee. Depending on how many employees are involved, participants could have a whole month's worth of challenges. Once all have been given and received, participants could prepare another ten and continue in the same way.

2.   Recommend that participants read biographies of those they consider outstanding leaders and/or visionaries. Once a month, members of the informal group could have lunch together and discuss what they heave learned about calculation-via-conjecture.

Questions for Further Consideration:

1.   What value can individuals derive from sharpening their imaginative reasoning abilities?

2.   What major changes do you see in your future? What preparations are you making so the transitions between current and future states will be facilitated?

3.   How much daydreaming do you do? Has it ever led to an improved state of affairs?

4.   What can you do to improve your imaginative-reasoning abilities?

Overview:	After being presented with an example, participants will apply the Five-Why technique to a current workplace problem and then to a situation involving recent news events.
Objective:	To afford practice with the Five-Why technique.
Supplies:	Copies of a recent news article, one per participant
Time:	About 20 minutes
Advance Preparation:	Make copies of a recent news report that invites in-depth analysis. If you can, arrange seating so table groups of five or six can work together.
Participants/ Application:	Any number of participants can work on this exercise, which works best as a mid-session or end-of-session skill-builder. By the halfway point in the course (or by the end), enough provocative questions or issues will have arisen to warrant the Five-Why application.

Introduction to Concept:

A popular problem-solving tool from the world of Total Quality Management (TQM) is the Five-Why technique. It has one person continuing to ask "Why?" until the root cause of a problem has been uncovered. This example shows how continued questioning helps us to analyze the multiple factors involved in problems, and not just the most obvious, most superficial ones.

William's variance report is late.

Why?

He's always playing catch-up.

Why?

He's been assigned to a two-week training program during the middle of budgets.

Why?

He really needs the training.

Why?

He was never given an orientation program when he was first hired.

Why?

I guess he just slipped through the cracks.

With this kind of probing, it is much easier to uncover the root cause of the problem. And that root cause, as we saw in William's case, may well go beyond the circumstances of the particular problem being investigated. While the lateness of a given report may be serious, more serious is the problem of employees not having the training they need to do the job *before* they start to do that job. The slipping-through-the-cracks problem is the long-term one that needs immediate attention.

Procedure:

1. Working in teams of five or six, participants will record problems that occur/exist in the workplace or in any other context they wish to address.

2. They will probe beneath the surface of the problem (as originally stated) to attempt to learn the real cause and, thus, what might be the real solution.

3. A representative (or two representatives, if there are only a few teams) from each team will meet with other representatives to prepare a report on what the various teams learned. As this special team is working, the remaining participants will work on a second exercise—applying the Five-Why technique to a recent news story in an effort to uncover beneath-the-surface causes for a given effect. Distribute the news story.

4. After 10 or 15 minutes, ask for the two reports: the first by a spokesperson for the special team and the second by a spokesperson from the team that discussed the recent news story.

Extending the Activity:

1. Invite a guest speaker (a senior manager, a community leader, a police officer) to address the class about a common problem. An appointed spokesperson from the class will ask (as professionally and diplomatically as possible) five "Why?" questions to get beneath surface discussions.

2. Ask participants to think about the last five major problems they solved or decisions they made. Have them discuss with one or two others the depth to which they probed beneath the surface to find root causes of the problems.

Workplace Connections:

1. Recommend that employees use the Five Why technique the next time they are tempted to hurl an accusation at a co-worker. Instead of jumping to conclusions and saying things they might later regret, participants can use the five "Why" questions as a means of exploring the problem instead of attacking the person with the problem.

2. Suggest that participants share this technique with their supervisors for future use.

Questions for Further Consideration:

1. What is causing some of the communication problems in your workplace?

2. Specifically, how should managers deal with employees who have problems?

3. What might be a negative result of such probing?

Overview: After exposure to two interesting problems, participants will employ the Force-Field Analysis to focus their thinking on resources that could be tapped in the process of solving a given problem.

Objective: To develop the use of analytical thinking via a structured format.

Supplies:
- Flipchart
- Marking pens in two different colors

Time: Approximately 25 minutes

Advance Preparation: Draw the Force Field Analysis (as shown in step 4 of the procedure) on the flipchart but keep it covered until the appropriate time.

Participants/ Application: This exercise works with any size group at any point when a cerebral energizer is needed. The exercise can be used to begin a session if a question like this is posed to the group: "What do you envision as the ideal state of affairs as far as [name topic of course you are facilitating] is concerned?" The analysis required by the Force Field Tool can also be related to various discussions that arise during the course of the day. If used as an end-of-session exercise, the question for the group would be, "Where do we go from here?" This question will lead to the broad division of forces (both restraining and driving) that will help participants achieve an ideal state.

Introduction to Concept:

Often, we fail to find the solutions we need because we fail to use the resources we have. We wear blinders, it seems, that prevent us from using what is right in front of us or right inside of us. Or we impose imaginary limits upon ourselves and assume that we are not allowed to proceed in a particular fashion. In truth, though, there are fewer rules or impediments than we think there are.

A good example of how available resources aren't always used to solve an important problem is this one involving a creative engineering class at M.I.T. The instructor had placed two ping-pong balls at the bottom of a metal cylinder, which was bolted to the floor of the science lab. The cylinder was about seven inches wide and about five feet high. The students had one full hour to remove the ping-pong balls from the cylinder. They could not leave the room but were free to use anything in the room. The professor encouraged them to work together, reminding them that if they found a solution, they would all pass the final exam and if they did not, they would all fail. They all failed. Had you been in that room, how would you have solved the problem? [Pause. Elicit solutions.]

Procedure:

1. The answer to the M.I.T. problem is "water," which students could have taken from the faucets in order to float the balls to the top. After challenging the class with the M.I.T. problem, ask participants to solve this next problem. [Note: It is important to set up this problem by using a colored magic marker to draw the lines and a different color to draw the letters.]

    In the following diagram, which letter does not belong?

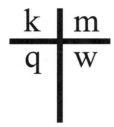

2. Call on various participants to explain their answers and then give the correct one: The letter "t," which most people don't even "see," is out of place because it is bigger, thicker, and of a different color than the other letters.

3. Psychologist Kurt Lewin devised a problem-solving tool that asks us to consider the current state of affairs and to juxtapose it with an ideal state of affairs. Having done that, we now consider what driving forces (indicated by a plus sign) will help us achieve the idealized state by using existing resources. Next, we think about the restraining forces (depicted by a minus sign) that may be preventing us from achieving the desired conditions.

4. Continue with this mini-lecture:

    The Force Field Analysis is depicted as a large "T," as you can see here. [Show diagram on flipchart.] *It's a valuable tool for analyzing a problem, ascertaining its causes, and evaluating the resources available for achieving the desired effect. An example of a problem that might be subject to such analysis is the illiteracy rate in America—1 out of 5 adults is functionally illiterate. That is the current status; ideally, there would be no such thing as illiteracy. The next step involves asking what forces could be used to bring us to the ideal state. Finally, we would consider what forces are causing the rate to be so high or keeping us from reaching the ideal. By reviewing the two columns, we can next decide the course of action that should be pursued.*

Current state: *20% illiteracy*	
Ideal state: *100% literacy*	
Driving Forces (+)	**Restraining Forces (-)**
government intervention *volunteer program* *public service ads* *athletes as mentors* *involvement of business* *community*	*busy lives* *too much television* *high dropout rates* *single parent homes* *immigration*

5. Divide the class into small groups of four or five and give each team a sheet of chart paper. Have each group identify a problem at the top of the chart paper and report its current and ideal states. The problem could be one currently facing them as businesspeople or all of us as a society.

6. Give each group another group's chart paper and ask members to list both the Driving and the Restraining forces for the problem listed.

7. After about 15 minutes, return the papers to the original groups and ask them to add further Driving and Restraining forces and then to select the one force (in either column) that—if they could direct their energies to it—they think could most effect the ideal solution.

8. Call on a spokesperson from each team to report on their selection.

Extending the Activity:

1. Have participants interview one another to learn what special talents/knowledge/abilities they have. Keep a classroom or corporate list of these resources and draw upon various individuals at various times for various projects.

2. Periodically do a brief force field analysis of issues raised by participants that relate to the subject matter of the course.

3. Begin the class with a large force field analysis addressing this issue: *"How can we maximize the investment in training, after the training?"* The current research is discouraging: Less than half of participants in training programs return to work and effect changes based on the new learning they have acquired. The ideal, of course, would be to have every participant put to use the new skills/concepts they acquired immediately after their return to the workplace.

4. Begin a collection of instances when slavish adherence to rules results in loss to an individual or organization. For example, after transferring to a new school in Seattle, a youngster asked his parents if he could go back to his old school. The reason for his request: The new school did not permit boys to work in the library. The no-boys rule meant considerable intellectual loss for the new school because… the fourth-grader who returned to View Ridge was none other than Bill Gates!

Workplace Connections:

1. If participants have not been asked by their supervisors, "What is the greatest contribution you can make to this organization?" encourage them to at least ask the question of co-workers or team members with whom they work.

2. We sometimes overlook available resources because we have not tapped the wealth of historical precedents. Suggest that participants study what has gone before in order to accomplish what is yet to be. In other words, what has been done in the past that might facilitate the solutions currently being sought or implemented?

Questions for Further Consideration:

1. What rules do you feel should be changed?

2. What do you think Tom Peters means when he says, "If you have gone a whole week without being disobedient, you are doing yourself and your organization a disservice?"

3. What resources—human and other—remain untapped in your organization?

4. Do you agree with author James Fixx, who asserts, "In solving puzzles, a self-assured attitude is half the battle?"

5. Kurt Lewin, originator of the Force Field Analysis method, has a model of change that calls for "Thawing," "Changing," and "Refreezing." Assume you wanted to make some positive change in the workplace. How, what, where, when, and possibly who would you thaw, change, and refreeze?

Overview:	"Autonomy of object" refers to the problem-solving process of making a problem come alive in order to find a possible solution. Participants will work in small groups to solve a problem of their own choosing in this manner.
Objective:	To provide participants with a problem-solving tool.
Supplies:	None required
Time:	Approximately 15 minutes
Advance Preparation:	Arrange the group, if logistics permit, into subgroups of five members.
Participants/ Application:	Because this exercise generates lively discussion, it works well as an ice-breaking activity. Applicable to any size group, it can also be used during the training session or at its conclusion. All that is needed for these last two applications would be a problem that arose naturally during the preceding training.

Introduction to Concept:

"Autonomy of object" is a technique requiring the problem-solver to actually personify the problem by placing it in the context of a different time or a different place. Interesting and novel solutions to the problem are frequently embedded within the mental associations we normally make with a particular era.

Let us say that graffiti is a problem in a given neighborhood. If the problem were personified, the graffiti might be seen as a bandit in the Wild West era. The Wild West might make you think of a "posse," and conceivably a posse would be formed to patrol the neighborhood looking for the offenders. This scenario might also make you think of sheriffs. By extension, then, perhaps the police could be asked to patrol more often than they currently do, or could be turned to for advice. Wild West–thinking might also lead you to badges, with their shiny, reflective surfaces. These thoughts could result in an invitation to a chemist to discuss chemicals that might be sprayed on select surfaces to deflect the paint.

Procedure:

1. Begin by listing numerous problems on the board or flipchart. Use problems related to workplace issues, if possible.

2. Prepare a second list, with input from participants, of various eras/locations different from the present. For each era and location, free-associate words related to those times and places.

3. Divide the class into small groups next and ask participants to select a problem and an era or location. They will then devise a possible solution by making the problem come alive (as was done with the graffiti-as-bandit situation).

4. Have the groups share their solutions.

Extending the Activity:

1. Have a current copy of the local newspaper available. Distribute a section or several pages to each group. Ask them to use the autonomy-of-object procedure to make the problem come alive and then to identify a lively solution for the problem.

2. Discuss the simple technique of *personification,* which makes an inanimate object come alive. Extend the discussion to workplace situations by asking participants to first list issues that concern them, and then to regard those issues from a new perspective by completing one or more of the following prompts:

> "If this problem could talk, it would say...."
> "If this problem could think, it would realize...."
> "If this problem could hear, it would have known...."
> "If this problem could create, it would have made...."
> "If this problem could be dressed, it would look like...."

Workplace Connections:

1. Ask a group of five supervisors/managers to volunteer to do the following: They will use the autonomy-of-object technique to ameliorate a workplace situation. Then, they will report back to their respective subordinates the success they had with the technique. If it worked well for them, encourage the supervisors to occasionally solve problems this way with their subordinates.

2. A genius has been defined as someone who shoots at something nobody else can see— and hits it. To generate this kind of visionary thinking, ask for a volunteer to call participants at least once during the next six months with this question, *"What are you looking at that no one else can see?"* To be sure, there are no guarantees that such prodding will result in lively solutions. But it may very well increase the number of invisible targets being hit.

Questions for Further Consideration:

1. The autonomy-of-object technique works because it stimulates thoughts we would not have had without the special context in which we place the problem. What other techniques do you know of to stimulate free association or brainstorming?

TEST OF CREATIVITY

A Self-Assessment Exercise

The left side of your brain handles analytical thinking: logical, rational, linear, numerical, precise. Many aspects of your job call for analytical thinking: planning a project, preparing a budget, learning a procedure, solving a problem, studying alternatives, and making decisions.

The right side of your brain handles creative thinking: expansive, visionary, intuitive, spatial, artistic. Whenever you come up with new ideas or create products, procedures, forms, programs, or plans that are new (or, at least, have never been generated by you before), you are drawing on the right side of your brain.

This self-assessment exercise will help you to get a quick measure of your creativity. There are fifteen questions. Each is timed. We suggest you get a kitchen timer or alarm clock or wristwatch, since you are likely to become absorbed in the exercises and forget to keep track of the time. Alternative: get a friend to be your timekeeper.

On each exercise, read the instructions. Then immediately start the clock.

1. **Five Minutes** In the space below (and on a separate sheet of paper if you need more space), list all the words you can think of that begin with the letter c. **Start timing now.**

2. The local soft drink bottling company has a fleet of trucks whose drivers make daily deliveries at the same supermarkets, drug stores, and beverage distributors. That is, the drivers visit all outlets on the routes every day.

   This July, the company noticed a higher than normal absenteeism on Fridays and Mondays. The drivers call in sick. This has meant that the route supervisors have had to drive the routes themselves. Since many drivers have exceeded their allowable sick days, the company is docking the drivers (i.e., not paying them) for absent days. But this has not reduced the absenteeism.

   (a) **Three Minutes** In the space below, list all the reasonable explanations you can think of as to why the drivers are calling in sick on Mondays and Fridays. **Start timing now.**

   (b) **Three Minutes** Assuming the explanations you just listed are valid, use the space below to list all the possible actions the bottling company might take to correct the problem. **Start timing now.**

3. **Three Minutes** A friend of yours manufactures peanut butter and other peanut products. Peanut shells are a by-product, and your friend has been carting them to the dump for use as landfill; they are, of course, biodegradable.

   You're convinced that the shells will have some commercial value if ways can be found to use them and not merely bury them. In the space below, list all the possible uses that you feel should be explored for their practicality. **Start timing now.**

4. **Three Minutes** Many fruits find their names used in figures of speech. For example, we refer to an unreliable automobile as a "lemon," or the boss or lead performer as the "top banana." In the space below, list all the figures of speech you can think of that include the name of a fruit. **Start timing now.**

5. Three Minutes It's scrabble time. Here are your seven letters. In the space below, see how many words you can assemble by using some of these letters (and no other letters). A letter may be used only once in each word. **Start timing now.**

NXEYOTI

Fifteen Minutes Complete as many of these assignments as you possibly can. Don't spend too much time on any that stump you. Move on to another. You can always return to an item if a new strategy or fresh insight comes to you. The exercise continues on the next page. **Start timing now.**

6. Describe how you could cut this piece of cheese into eight equal pieces with only three cuts.

    Answer:_____

    _____

    _____

    _____

7. Join the nine dots shown at the right by drawing four straight lines without lifting your pencil from the paper.

    Then do the same for the nine dots shown below by drawing three straight lines without lifting your pencil.

8. By drawing one line, convert this odd number into an even number.

IX

9. You have a 5-minute hourglass and a 3-minute hourglass. You want to measure 7 minutes. How?

Answer: _____

_____

_____

10. How many squares are there in this figure?

1	5	9	13
2	6	10	14
3	7	11	15
4	8	12	16

Answer: _____

11. What do the following words have in common?

canopy, deft, first, laughing, hijack, stupid, calmness, labcoat

Answer: _____

_____

12. Add lines to the two identical figures at the right to convert them into three-letter abbreviations for two world-famous organizations.

These organizations are: _____

_____

_____

13. Nine wolves are in this square enclosure at the zoo. Draw two more square enclosures that will put each wolf in a pen by itself.

14. What is the logic behind this sequence of the numbers one through nine?

8, 5, 4, 9, 1, 7, 6, 3, 2

Answer: _____

_____

_____

15.

Three cans are full and three are empty. By moving only one can, see if you can end up with full and empty cans alternating.

Answer: _____

_____

_____

ANALYTICAL THINKING TEST
A Self-Assessment Exercise

Directions: There are two parts to this exercise. In Part One, you'll be reading five situations, each followed by four conclusions. Some conclusions are true (T), some are false (F), and some are questionable or cannot be made without further information (?). Beside each conclusion, indicate which applies by placing an X over the appropriate answer.

PART ONE

1. According to the police in the suburban town of Maplewood, the automobile accidents occurring during the workweek (Monday through Friday) are 250% more numerous than those occurring during the weekend (Saturday and Sunday). We can conclude that:

    A. Traffic at commuter hours is probably contributing to the higher workweek accident rate............................ | T | ? | F |

    B. Accidents are as likely during the workweek as on the weekend... | T | ? | F |

    C. It's more dangerous for you to drive during the workweek than on weekends in Maplewood.................. | T | ? | F |

    D. Maplewood may not be a commuter community.. | T | ? | F |

2. George is a recent MBA who wishes to spend a year working overseas. He understands that the newly independent nation of Rotunda needs MBAs, both in government and private industry. Salaries are paid in Rotunda Dollars (RD). The range paid to MBAs is from 7,000 to 21,000 RD per annum, depending on experience. Half the MBAs earn less than 14,000 RD and half earn more than 14,000 RD. From this we conclude that:

    A. The average salary of MBAs in Rotunda is 14,000 RD.. | T | ? | F |

    B. A normal distribution (bell-shaped curve) seems to apply here .... | T | ? | F |

    C. The chances are 50-50 that George will earn more than 14,000 RD in his first year........................... | T | ? | F |

    D. MBAs in Rotunda typically earn between 12,000 and 16,000 RD .... | T | ? | F |

3. A group of surveyors who wanted to find out the fuel oil consumption for residential heating in 1985 throughout the state of Pennsyltucky interviewed a representative sample of homeowners by telephone in early 1986, asking the following question: "What would you say is the average monthly amount of fuel oil used to heat your home last year?" The results yielded a statewide average of 47.3 gallons of No. 2 fuel oil per month. From this we know that:

A. The question should have asked for the annual amount of fuel oil used to heat their home .... | T | ? | F |

B. Telephoning people and asking them to guess is a poor way to obtain the desired information .... | T | ? | F |

C. The average Pennsyltucky home will require about 567.6 gallons of oil for heat in 1986 .... | T | ? | F |

D. Apartment dwellers were excluded from the survey .... | T | ? | F |

4. A major automotive dealership mailed a questionnaire to all customers who had purchased a new car within the prior year. The questionnaire asked, among other things, whether they would like to have received a free check-up every 5000 miles during the six months following purchase. Of the 27% who responded, 68% stated that they were in favor of having a free check-up. From this we can conclude that:

A. A majority of new car owners who had purchased through this dealership favored having a free check-up.. | T | ? | F |

B. With regard to the sample, the number of respondents may be adequate, but their representativeness may not be .... | T | ? | F |

C. The dealership believes that free check-ups during the half year following purchase of a new car are desirable .... | T | ? | F |

D. The percentages would probably have been different if the survey had involved respondents who purchased two or more new cars .... | T | ? | F |

5. Grassmaster, a lawn mower manufacturer, must select a supplier of paint that will dry within 20 minutes of spraying. Two vendors have been identified for consideration: A and B. Paint from A dries slower than B's paint at normal room temperature (68°F). But at temperatures of 90°F and higher, A's paint dries faster than B's. Both dry at the same rate when equal amounts of Agent X are added to the paints during the normal manufacturing process. Agent X is already present in B's product as part of the normal manufacturing process, but not in A's. From this we can conclude that:

A. Grassmaster could buy A's paint as normally manufactured and add Agent X before spraying it in order to shorten the drying time .... `T | ? | F`

B. Two factors affect drying time: heat (room temperature) and Agent X .... `T | ? | F`

C. As long as Agent X is present in paint, the drying time is reduced. The amount is unimportant .... `T | ? | F`

D. Agent X exerts a greater influence on drying time than does room temperature .... `T | ? | F`

PART TWO

Directions: There are three proposals (A, B, and C) stated below. You are to select one of these three and develop a list of all the advantages and disadvantages (pros and cons) of implementing it, as well as all the interesting points associated with the proposal (further information to be obtained before or after the proposal is acted upon). Complete the table on the next page for the proposal you select. Go for quantity—the more entries you have in each column, the better will be your chances of thinking clearly when you decide whether to recommend that the proposal be accepted or rejected. Here are the three proposals, from which you should now select one and complete the table on the next page.

A. Proposed: That state laws be passed requiring that a man and a woman desiring to marry must first announce their engagement in the local newspaper and then live together for a minimum of three months before applying for a marriage license.

B. Proposed: That all young men and women be required to serve one summer in the army in military training; this requirement would be to serve for 10 weeks at any point between their 17th and their 20th birthday.

C. Proposed: That each citizen of the country receive from the government a plastic laminated identification card containing their photo, signature, and identification number (Social Security number in the U.S.), to be carried or worn at all times.

After selecting the proposal you will be thinking through, develop your list by using the table on the next page.

ADVANTAGES	DISADVANTAGES	INTERESTING POINTS

TEST OF CREATIVITY

Answer Sheet and Feedback

The test you just completed covers the major types of mental activity associated with creativity: insight, recognizing relationships that are not easily evident, visualizing, thinking laterally as well as linearly, withholding evaluation (judgment) so as to generate many ideas (brainstorming), using familiar concepts or objects in unfamiliar (novel) ways, and so on.

Creative people tend to have traits that are not shared by most other people. Often they have grown up as "loners," seeking solitude rather than friends and peer group support. They see no reason to conform and meet arbitrary norms. They value their uniqueness and originality. They are not ashamed of having "off-the-wall" thoughts and do not fear the realization that others will see them as bizarre, foolish, or "out-of-touch." They prefer challenge to routine, and value excitement over predictability and fixedness.

Although creativity requires superior intelligence, a high I.Q. is no guarantee of creativity. In fact, only a small fraction of the intellectually gifted are creative. Besides being novel, the fruits of your creativity must also be appropriate or relevant or satisfying to others (for example, aesthetically pleasing in works of art or music). Otherwise, anyone who smears paint on canvas or pounds on piano keys in novel and bizarre ways would have to be deemed creative (and this could include the entire family of man as well as our primate friends, apes, monkeys, and King Kong!).

1. On this first exercise, your mission was to come up with as many words as you can generate in five minutes that begin with the letter c. Did you plunge right in by listing any word that came to mind? Or did you spend a moment planning your creative journey with questions like these:

   (a) Is it better to work through the alphabet so as to avoid later confusion as to whether you've already used a word (e.g., all "ca . . ." words, followed by all "ce . . ." words, "ch . . ." words, etc.)?

   (b) Is it better to write only one-syllable words, since you can write more of them in three minutes (e.g., can, cow, cut, chip versus circumference, communications, celebrity)?

   (c) Is it acceptable to use different forms of the same word (e.g., cheat, cheater, cheats, cheating), or would that not be very challenging or original? (Remember: creative people prefer challenge and excitement to routine and fixedness.)

All of these questions are rational and analytical, and draw on the left brain. Creative individuals harness and channel their creativity by planning their approach to a creative assignment with such questions. If you did so, you probably realize that: (a) an alphabetic approach would enable you to generate more words in shorter time, since you are following a system rather than a random process; (b) although one-syllable words can be written more quickly, if you start to pass judgment and edit yourself, your momentum will slow down; (c) if you are highly creative, you're likely to be bored by simply sticking different endings onto a root word. You won't see them as new (original, novel) words, and there won't be much challenge or excitement.

Printed below is a list of c words to show how easy it is to follow these (a), (b), (c) guidelines and to generate words as fast as you can write. Writing at a rate of 30 words per minute, you could come up with about 150 words, as shown in the list below. (No need for your list to resemble ours, of course.) Take a moment to count the total number of words you generated in five minutes. Divide this number by five.

Enter the resulting number in the box at the right (total divided by five) ☐ **1**

CA	cab, cache, cad, cadmium, cadet, cadaver, cafe, cage, cake, calf, caliber, cam, came, can, cane, cap, caper, cape, capillary, car, carnage, carpet, care, carry carrot, carp, case, cast, castle, caste, cat, catch, cater, cattle, cataract, cave, caveat, cavity
CE	cedar, ceiling, certain, celebrity, celery, cell, celtic, cement, cemetery, censor, census, centennial, century, cent, centimeter
CH	chap, char, chat, chant, chair, chablis, chafing, charge, chastise, chapter, charity, chatterbox, cheap, cheat, cheer, chest, check, chef, chip, chicle, chic, chin, chirp, chit, chisel, chimney, chimp, chive, choke, chow, chock, chore, chose, chunk, chute
CI	cigar, cilia, cinder, circle, circumference, circumvent, cistern, city, civics, civil
CL	clone, claw, clasp, cliff, clique, clump, clip, clown, clutch, clef, clean, clear, cloud, clout
CO	cord, con, (convent, convex, convert, control . . . etc.) corn, cob, cod, coffee, cog, cogitate, coke, cold, color, collate, collide, cop, copper, cope, core, cot, cottage, coddle, cove, covey, cover, cow, cower, coy, coyote, cozy
CR	crap, crate, crash, cranberry, crazy, crest, cream, crisp, criterion, croak, crown, crow, croon, crock, crouton, crud, cruller, crust, cruet, cruel
CU	cub, cuckoo, cuckold, cud, cuddle, cue, cuff, culinary, culprit, cull, cunning, cup, cur, curt, curdle, curfew, curate, cure, cusp, cuss, custard, cut, cute
CY	cymbal, cyst, cynic, cycle, cyclical

2. In this exercise, you generated possible explanations in response to (a), then came up with possible solutions in response to (b). We've listed twelve relevant answers to each. Your responses will differ from ours, of course. See how many plausible responses you came up with.

Enter your total to parts (a) and (b) in the box at the right.

2

(a)
- it's summer and they value their three- to four-day weekends more than the money
- they really are sick, having exerted themselves excessively over the weekend
- they have Monday hangovers
- they are paid so well that the docking doesn't hurt them
- the Friday deliveries are heavier: more work stocking stores for the weekend
- the Monday "out-of-stocks" (it's summer) mean more work and second trips
- the routes are too big, too many outlets
- the traffic on Friday and Monday is too much of a hassle
- weekend sporting events (stadium, arena, coliseum) require much more labor
- their trucks can't carry enough product for extra-heavy Monday/Friday deliveries
- their jobs aren't satisfying; long weekends are providing the balance
- drivers may be going off in groups for long weekends (hunting, fishing, drinking)

(b)
- provide weekend deliveries for stores that have had "out-of-stock" conditions
- take advance orders by phone so trucks carry only what they need
- reduce the number and variety of packages (sizes, cans vs. bottles)
- hire helpers to work with drivers; they can run routes if necessary
- have retirees on call in case regulars don't show up
- carry more product: use larger trucks or use pallets for delivery to larger stores
- increase the penalty for absenteeism
- reapportion the territory so as to break up larger (out-of-stock) routes
- set up a special weekend "hot line" so that dealers can phone for supplementary delivery
- terminate for excessive absenteeism, replace with drivers with a different work ethic
- deliver product to sporting events during midweek, not on Friday
- carry only the best sellers on Monday and Friday (80% of sales come from 20% of product line)

3. Creativity requires superior intelligence. In this exercise, you could channel your thinking into a variety of different fields: agriculture, construction, manufacture, and so on. Your ability to "shift gears" and move your focus from one context to another is important to success on exercises such as this.

First of all, you should recognize that peanut shells can be used "as is" in some applications. However, by processing them, we can greatly expand our list of potential uses, as shown in the list below. We've listed 15 applications—many more than you had time to generate or write in 3 minutes.

Enter your total in the box at the right.

☐ 3

Use peanut shells "as is" for:

- animal feed (silage)
- filler in human food (like soybeans)
- aggregate (additive) in cement for use as stucco—makes it lighter
- fiber in "scratch coat" (undercoat) prior to fine plaster coat
- fiber in asphalt as paving
- pulp to be rolled into special kinds of paper or sheet products
- insulation (if fireproofing is economical or unnecessary)
- additive in potting soil—helps it breathe
- filler in a contained jumping, rolling, bouncing area for children
- filler (sterilized) in pillows, quilts, blankets (like kapok)

Process the shells (shred, grind, pulverize) to use as:

- mulch and ground cover for planting areas
- fuel, either alone or as additive
- packing material (like styrofoam pellets and squiggles)
- crushable filler in highway and vehicle collision barriers (in bags or plastic canisters)
- additive to plastic, resins, plaster, cement (fibers add strength)

4. If English is not your native language, you will find an exercise like this to be especially challenging. Let's see how the fruits of your labor compare with ours. Listed below are some candidates for "fruity" figures of speech.

Enter your total in the box at the right.

☐ 4

grapes of wrath	they gave him the raspberry	a blueberry sky
sour grapes	life is a bowl of cherries	that soldier is a cherry
that car is a lemon	turn lemons into lemonade	the apple of her daddy's eye
his new job is a plum	a banana republic	heard it through the grapevine
a peach of a deal	apple polishing is brownnosing	the pineapple failed to detonate
a strawberry blonde	he's a real slick apple	the crowd went bananas
a hot tomato	a strawberry mark on her thigh	he painted it lime (orange, plum)

5. Words formed from these letters are listed below. Note the flow, or sequence in which the mind can be mapped to go from each word to the next. This helps in identifying the full range of possibilities, or as many as 3 minutes will allow.

NXEYOTI

Enter your total in the box at the right.

☐ 5

ONYX	TEX	YET	TONE	ON	EN	ONE	TEN
EXIT	NIX	YIN	NOTE	NO	ET	EON	TOE
OX	NEXT	YON	NOT	TO	IT	TIE	TOY
OXEN	NET	TON	NIT	YO	TI	TIN	TONY

6. Cut the cheese horizontally into two equal cakes. Then cut vertically into four equal 90° wedges.

7. You must go outside the area of the nine dots to solve each puzzle.

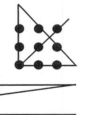

8.

SIX

One line will convert a Roman number nine into a six.

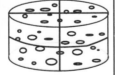

9. Start both glasses simultaneously. When the three runs out, two minutes will remain on the five-minute timer. As soon as the two minutes run out, turn the glass over.

2 + 5 = 7

10. 16 individual squares
  4 corner quadrants (e.g., 1, 2, 5, 6)
  1 middle square (6, 7, 10, 11)
  4 arms of a cross (e.g., 2, 3, 6, 7)
  4 corners 3x3 (e.g., 1,2,3, 5,6,7, 9,10,11)
  1 biggest square (4x4 squares)
  $\overline{30}$
	11. Each of these words contains three successive letters of the alphabet:
	nop in canopy, def in deft, rst in first, etc.

12. *USA* *USN* United States of America, or U.S. Army United States Navy	13.
14. Their names are in alphabetic order: **Eight, Five, Four, Nine, One, Seven, Six, Three, Two**	15. Pour the contents of the middle full bucket into the middle empty bucket.

Give yourself two points for each of the ten assignments that you got right. Give one point for half-right answers. The total possible is 20 points.

Enter your total in the box at the right.

6–15

HOW DID YOU DO?

Highly creative persons will usually score in the range of 15–20 points in each of the six boxes, for a total of 90–120 points. Moderately creative persons typically score in the range of 10–15 points on each item, for a total of 60–90 points. Add up your scores in the six boxes, and enter this new total in the box at the right.

What insights have you gained into the nature of creativity and your areas of creative strength and weakness?

ANALYTICAL THINKING TEST
Answer Sheet

Directions: The correct answers are noted below, along with the reasons. Place a check mark beside every answer you got correct. There is a total of 20 points possible. Enter your score in this box ....

PART ONE

1. Automobile accidents in Maplewood

A. False. The accident rate is not higher during the workweek. Even if this is a commuter town (which we don't know), workweek accidents are as frequent as weekend ones.. | T | ? | ☒ |

B. True, since 250% is 2.5 times, and days are also 2.5 times as numerous in the workweek as on weekends... | ☒ | ? | F |

C. We cannot tell until we define "dangerous," which depends on when (hour of the day) and where (commuting, shopping, etc.) you're driving .... | T | ☒ | F |

D. True. (It would also be true if the statement said that Maplewood might be a commuter community.) .... | ☒ | ? | F |

2. Annual salaries for MBAs in Rotunda

A. We don't know this. If the distribution is normal, this would be true. But we cannot assume that income is distributed normally between 7,000 and 21,000 RD.............. | T | ☒ | F |

B. We don't know this. There might be two distinct income groups, new vs. experienced, natives vs. mother country, government vs. private industry (i.e., a "bimodal" distribution).. | T | ☒ | F |

C. This is not an issue of chance. George is a recent MBA, and pay is based on experience. George's first-year earnings are likely to be less than 14,000 RD.......... | T | ? | ☒ |

D. True if distribution is normal, false if distribution is bimodal. Since we don't know, we must question the statement .... | T | ☒ | F |

3. Fuel oil consumption throughout Pennsyltucky

A. True. People are more likely to remember annual consumption than "average monthly." Also, the time of year of the survey may affect "monthly" estimates........... | ☒ | ? | F |

B. True. Fuel oil distributors could provide more accurate information and with much less effort by the researchers .... | ☒ | ? | F |

C. We don't know enough to forecast. The research is shaky, the weather varies, and the 12-times-multiplier can turn small errors into large ones........................... | T | ☒ | F |

D. True. Only homeowners were contacted. Some apartment dwellers might own their own apartments (condo, co-op, etc.), but some others don't own, making the statement true.. | ☒ | ? | F |

4. Free check-up for new car purchases

    A. If it had read "majority of respondents," then the statement would be true. But we need more than a 27% response to generalize to "majority of new car owners.".......

    B. True. Each part is true. Even if the first part had read ". . . may *not* be adequate," it would still be true. Similarly, the second part is true whether it reads "may be" or "may not be." In fact, we have reason to suspect that the respondents are not representative, since those not interested in a free check-up are less likely to reply than those favoring it. .....

    C. It is risky to infer motives from the dealer's actions. Also, we don't know what "desirable" means. From a vehicle maintenance standpoint, yes (true). From a profitability standpoint, no (false).............

    D. False. The survey was not limited to purchases of only one new car. Those who purchased two or more new cars are already involved as respondents....................

5. Grassmaster's need for fast-drying paint

    A. We don't know if adding Agent X after manufacture will have the same effect as adding it during manufacture ....

    B. True. There may be other factors that also affect drying time, but the statement is still true as it stands ....

    C. We don't know if there are upper and lower limits to the amount of Agent X necessary for it to speed up drying time ....

    D. False. Room temperature (90°F) exerted a greater influence on drying time than did the presence of Agent X ....

Reminder: Count the total number of answers you got correct and enter this number in the box on the previous page. Then go on to Part Two.

PART TWO

There are no right or wrong answers to the exercise you went through. However, you should have come up with at least five advantages, five disadvantages, and two or three interesting points. These numbers should double when the list is expanded as a group activity. Here are our lists, with which you can compare your own.

A. Couples desiring marriage must first live together for three months:

ADVANTAGES	DISADVANTAGES	INTERESTING POINTS
1. Fewer surprises and risk of marriage not working.	1. Could lead some people to becoming "marriage samplers," living with different mates but never marrying.	1. What would be the view of the churches and religious leaders?
2. Reduced divorce rate.		2. Where would couples live together?
3. Couples learn how to live together in a relatively "fail-safe" environment—less pressure.	2. Buying or renting a home or apartment will be expensive if marriage doesn't materialize (leases are for more than three months).	3. What effect on abortion rate?
4. Fewer "passion" marriages.		4. What effect on divorce rate?
5. Eliminate marriages done for legal reasons and not for love (e.g., to gain entry to U.S., to qualify for an inheritance, etc.).	3. Some might enter it just to have a child more "legitimately."	5. Is three months enough to accomplish the purpose of the proposal?
6. Supportiveness of parents and friends can be determined and possibly influenced before marriage.	4. Psychologically damaging by creating "losers" who have been through several engagements without marriage.	
7. Psychology of "building toward" is more constructive than "after the honeymoon."	5. Difficult for some partners who know they want marriage now and cannot wait three months (e.g., military or student far away from their would-be spouse, dying person wanting to marry nurse).	
8. Young couples who don't understand implications and responsibilities of marriage would enter it with more maturity.		
9. Stimulates business in the apartment-rental industry.	6. Couples who have grown up together ("the girl next door") and known each other for years shouldn't have to live together before marrying.	
10. Public announcement of intent reduces the temptation to "play the field" during the months preceding marriage.	7. If they make it through the tryout period, it's not necessarily smooth sailing thereafter.	

ADVANTAGES	DISADVANTAGES	INTERESTING POINTS
	8. Unnecessary—couples who want to live together before marriage (or even without marriage) can already do so without any need to formalize or legalize the procedure. 9. Newspapers will become crammed with engagement notices—not very interesting reading. 10. Successful tryouts might lead couples to continue to live together and never marry.	

B. Youths would be required to serve one summer (10 weeks) in the army:

ADVANTAGES	DISADVANTAGES	INTERESTING POINTS
1. Eliminate the need for draft for longer period (1–2 years). 2. Develop physical and mental stamina, self-reliance, discipline, respect for authority, pride in serving country, etc. 3. Reaches many youth when they are least influenced by parents, teachers, and other "authority figures." 4. Provides another set of role models for shaping values to live by. 5. Enables youth of all socio-economic levels and sub-cultures to live and work together in a relatively fail-safe environment. 6. Time (10 weeks) is long enough to effect permanent position change, yet short enough to not be disruptive to lives (education, career, marriage, etc.). 7. Give the country a trained citizen's army that is relatively combat-ready at any time; serves as deterrent to other nations taking military action against us. 8. Gives all youth an equal view of what a career in the military would be like, probably leading to more career soldiers. 9. Better quality of recruits than in present army. 10. Increase in patriotism, and a better informed electorate.	1. Disruptive to personal lives. 2. Seen as curtailment of individual freedom. 3. Expensive to give everyone a little instead of giving a few trainees a lot (breadth vs. depth). 4. Might require additional military bases, equipment, training cadre, etc. 5. Would they really be combat-ready, or would they *think* they were fit to fight, especially against a professional, full-time army? 6. Hard to administer and determine at what age each youth will attend, and when. 7. Many weapons and defense systems are too high-tech to be operated by people who have only had ten weeks of basic training. 8. Likely to create a caste system of "regulars" and "10-week wonders." 9. Difficult administering the exceptions who are excused for such things as for physical or mental disabilities. 10. U.S. could become subject of international ridicule.	1. Would all youths get the same training for 10 weeks? Or would there be different tracks? 2. Should they live on a military base, or could they live at home and commute to a nearby base? 3. Could efficiency of military training be improved, given the higher level of trainees? 4. How many people are we talking about each summer? 5. Would trainees be harassed or required to perform menial chores that might negate many of the advantages?

C. Government issuance of a photo-signature plastic I.D. to all citizens:

ADVANTAGES	DISADVANTAGES	INTERESTING POINTS
1. Is highly reliable I.D. for check cashing, travel, etc.	1. More costly than I.D. number only.	1. How often would this be done—every 10–20 years?
2. Should reduce fraud and similar criminal acts.	2. People wanting "newer" photos every few years.	2. Where done—at Post Offices? Motor vehicle registries?
3. Is more personal than just a number.	3. Requires equipment (Polaroid camera, laminator).	3. Would people carry them? Would laws be necessary requiring this (like the wearing of seat belts)?
4. Makes census-taking more accurate.	4. Requires operators and training in how to operate the equipment.	4. How long would citizens have to wait during the initial "tidal wave" of issuing cards to every Social Security card holder?
5. Would establish drinking age reliably.	5. Cannot be done by mail— citizen must go to a center.	
6. Provides better control of illegal immigration.	6. Citizens annoyed by the inconvenience, the unflattering photo.	5. Could this be alleviated via alphabetic scheduling (e.g., all A through C names during the first two weeks of August, etc.)?
7. Time saved in establishing positive I.D. over one's lifetime should more than offset the time and cost of going in for a photo.	7. Replacement of lost cards a nuisance and expense.	
8. Police have an immediate check on drivers of stolen vehicles, contraband, etc.	8. Fraud still possible through makeup, wigs, eyeglasses, moustaches, etc.	
9. Could eliminate need for passports or visas to some countries.	9. Could add employees to government payroll instead of reducing costs.	
10. Government could charge and make money on it.	10. Some people change in physical appearance much faster than others.	

Bibliography

Adams, James. *Conceptual Blockbusting.* New York: Addison-Wesley, 1986.

Albrecht, Karl. *Brain Power.* New York: Prentice-Hall, Inc., 1980.

Armstrong, David. *Managing by Storying Around.* New York: Doubleday, 1992.

Bennis, Warren, and Burt Nanus. *Leaders: The Strategies for Taking Charge.* New York: Harper & Row, 1985.

Bridge, William. *Job Shift.* New York: Addison-Wesley, 1995.

Campbell, David. *Take the Road to Creativity and Get Off Your Dead End.* Greensboro: Center for Creative Leadership, 1977.

Drucker, Peter. *The Effective Executive.* New York: Harper & Row, 1985.

Foster, Richard. *Innovation.* New York: Simon & Schuster, 1986.

Hammer, Michael, and James Champy. *Reengineering the Corporation.* New York: HarperCollins, 1993.

Imai, Masaaki. *Kaizen.* New York: Random House, 1986.

Kriegel, Robert. *If It Ain't Broke, Break It!* New York: Time Warner, 1991.

McClelland, David. *Some Social Consequences of Achievement Motivation.* New York: Irvington Publishers, Inc., 1993.

Munk, Nina, and Suzanne Oliver. "Think Fast." *Forbes* magazine, Volume 160, Number 3, March 24, 1997, pages 146–151.

Naisbitt, John, and Patricia Aburdene. *Megatrends 2000.* New York: William Morrow & Company, 1990.

Nelson, Robert. *1001 Ways to Reward Employees.* New York: Workman Publishers, 1994.

Norins, Hanley. *Traveling Creative Workshop.* New York: Prentice-Hall, Inc., 1990.

Quinlivan-Hall, David, and Peter Renner. *In Search of Solutions.* Vancouver: PFR Training Associates Limited, 1990.

Ruggiero, Vincent. *The Art of Thinking.* New York: Harper & Row, 1988.

Stack, Jack. *The Great Game of Business.* New York: Doubleday, 1992.

Thompson, Charles. *What a Great Idea.* New York: HarperCollins, 1992.

Wallenchinsky, David, and Amy Wallace. *The Book of Lists.* New York: Little, Brown and Company, 1993.